# PARTNERS
## *in marriage & ministry*

## A Biblical Picture of Gender Equality

Ronald W. Pierce

**Christians for Biblical Equality**
cbeinternational.org

*Partners in Marriage and Ministry*

© 2011 by Ronald W. Pierce

Published by Christians for Biblical Equality
122 W Franklin Ave, Suite 218
Minneapolis, MN 55404
cbeinternational.org

All Scripture quotations are the author's own translation or paraphrase, unless otherwise noted.

All references to the NIV are to the 2010 revision: THE HOLY BIBLE, NEW INTERNATIONAL VERSION®, NIV® Copyright © 1973, 1978, 1984, 2010 by Biblica, Inc.™ Used by permission. All rights reserved worldwide.

Design: Megan Greulich
Cover image: DorianGray/IStockphoto

ISBN-13: 978-0-9820465-2-4

Printed in the United States of America

Library of Congress Control Number: 2011925007

*For Pat, my partner for over forty years. She shares with me God's gracious gift of life.*

# CONTENTS

# Personal Journeys

*Why should this concern me?*

Perhaps you're a young woman who senses a call to serve God in Christian ministry and you've been told that there are some areas of service off limits to you because of your gender. Or, you are thinking about getting married but have heard that you must be willing to let your future husband "take the lead" in spiritual matters, as well as make the final decision on any disagreements. After all, you're told, husbands are responsible before God for their wives and children.

On the other hand, it could be that you're a man looking at these questions from a different perspective. You may have heard from your pastor that God wants men to be the leaders in both home and church. Moreover, for you to shirk this calling would be a sin. Yet, bearing such a burden feels too heavy for you personally — even something for which you feel unfit or inadequate.

You might be a parent whose son or daughter has had an experience like these and is coming to you for advice. They tell you that they've read the passages in the Bible about men and women, but some seem unclear. Or, perhaps these texts don't speak specifically to the questions they are facing. They have consulted evangelical scholars on the subject through books and seminars, but even there they found significant disagreements.

Maybe your church has suffered division and hurt over this issue to some degree — possibly even a major split in the congregation. Or, a group is suggesting that the church consider a woman for a place on the elder board — or even for a high-level pastoral position. You don't know what to do, or which side to take. You want women to be all that God desires for them, but you simply don't know who or what to believe.

Do any of these scenarios sound familiar? If so, you've got good reason to care about how men and women relate in marriage and ministry. If you are a believer in Jesus Christ and therefore part of Christ's body, the church, this issue will impact your life, as well as the lives of other believers — your sisters and brothers in Christ. In marriage, it will affect your relationship with your spouse and children. If you remain single, it will still shape the way you think of, and relate to, other women and men within your circle of friends. If you share in the responsibility of appointing godly and gifted leaders in your church — as you should — you will be faced with deciding how gender affects this process. And so on. The gender question touches every aspect of life, because God created people to relate to each other as male and female.

## *What's in your suitcase?*

We all bring a certain degree of "baggage" with us when we read the Bible or discuss theology. Perhaps you recognize some of your own "stuff" reflected in the questions above? I do! And though I can't peek into your suitcase as I'm writing this book, you may be helped by ideas I've collected along the way on my journey regarding this issue.

I grew up in a traditional Christian family in the 1950s. My father was expected to be the leader and provider, while my mother was to be the homemaker who reared the children (six of us). And, we generally assumed that men should take the lead in the small Brethren church we attended in rural Pennsylvania.

Years later, when my wife Pat and I married in 1969, there was an unspoken assumption that I would give leadership to our relationship and accept the responsibilities that came with "the man's role." It was the only model we had witnessed in our respective homes. The arrangement seemed to work fairly well. More importantly, we thought it was biblical, although neither of us had really studied the issue.

I did not begin to study the Bible in earnest regarding this topic until my first year of teaching Bible and theology at a Christian college in Southern California in the mid-1970s. It was a tumultuous era in the wake of the secular movement for racial and gender equality that had reached a boiling point in the 1960s.

The topic of gender "roles" came up naturally in a class I taught at that time on the biblical idea of "church." Soon it became an area of special interest that I've chosen to address regularly ever since. I teamed up recently with twenty-five other biblical and theological scholars to publish a full-length academic text on the subject, called *Discovering Biblical Equality* (InterVarsity, 2005). In addition, I've spoken at schools, churches, conferences, debates, and dialogues for over twenty-five years. Gender equality remains a major emphasis in my thinking, research, writing, and personal life.

This study eventually led me down a road that has not always been predictable. Nor has it continued in the same direction. Both my background and the era in which I lived forced me to search the Scriptures like the ancient Bereans (Acts 17:11) to rethink the position I had taken for granted for so long. In the end, I discovered that the Bible teaches a shared relationship of mutuality, an equal though diverse partnership between women and men in both marriage and ministry.

Yes, God created humanity as male and female in the divine image. And, as such, we have innate and beneficial differences. But, I can find no evidence in Scripture that God intended for only one to lead and the other to follow. Rather, the unity and diversity shared by men and women should be characterized by mutual submission in the body of Christ—in both the church and the home.

## *What's on the agenda?*

Several principles have guided me in writing this book. First and foremost, I have sought to base my writing on the Bible, to which I personally submit as the fully inspired and authoritative Word of God. This principle will be evident from the eight main chapters, which focus on key passages relating to this important topic. It can also be seen in the many other biblical references made throughout the chapters. I trust that you'll have your Bible open as you read this book in order to see these texts in their larger contexts. As a colleague and friend of mine, Ed Curtis, once said, "If we stick to what Scripture clearly teaches — that is, where evangelicals can agree — we'll have more on our plates than we can say grace over!"

Second, my heart's desire is to approach this question in a positive and unifying way. I want to emphasize more of what we as evangelicals share in common, rather than what divides us. Jesus prayed to the Father on our behalf saying, "Sanctify them by the truth; your word is truth...that all of them may be one...so that they may be brought to complete unity. Then the world will know that you sent me" (John 17:17–23). Jesus calls us to both truth and unity.

Third, I have tried to make this book practical. The great pastor and preacher Charles Swindoll used to say, "Some teachers take a simple idea and make it so complex that only other scholars can understand it. In contrast, a good teacher takes a complex idea and makes it clear enough so everyone can understand." With this in mind, I have grouped the key passages into three larger sections: the theological foundation (section one), marriage (section two), and ministry (section three). Each section ends with a summary of some challenging "Principles for Today."

Fourth, I have made every effort to be concise. The old Jewish rabbi Hillel was once asked to answer a question while his student "stood on one foot." In other words, "Give me the short version!" I get this kind of request frequently at the university where I teach and the church where my wife, Pat, and I minister as laypersons — and to some degree it is legitimate. We live harried lives in a fast-paced world trying to make ends meet. This book is an overview of the big picture, the biblical essentials of mutual partnership as men and women. If you'd like to do further study, a short reference list is provided at the end.

Finally, I have not held back from being passionate. The concluding chapter, "Paths to the Future," will show where I believe my journey is leading. This journey is to a better place, to a place of greater hope than we now face. And, it is a journey that we as believers can and must take together. It is a journey for passionate servants of Christ.

# PARTNERS
## *from Creation to the Cross*

# — 1 —

# Discovering God's Good Creation
### *Genesis 1-3*

In the thirty plus years that I have researched, taught, and written on the Bible and theology, I've developed a deep love for the Old Testament, especially its narratives. And, since God has chosen to begin the Bible with the creation stories, we will start there also.

Two complementary creation accounts appear in Genesis, with chapter one laying the foundation for chapter two. The theme of Genesis 1-2 together is human beings fashioned in God's image as male and female. The subject of gender is at the very center of the creative event that begins the entire story of Scripture.

## *What does it mean to be created in God's image?*

> In the beginning God created humanity in his own image as male and female. Then, he blessed them saying, "Have children and populate the earth — rule over all its creatures" (Gen. 1:26–28).

When I first began to study the creation accounts I got a surprise. Ordinary people like you and me are presented as the crowning achievement of God's creation. We might have expected the extraordinary beauties of the earth or fathomless wonders of the universe. But instead, God chose human beings fashioned in the divine image as male and female. Indeed we were designed to be in a personal, intimate relationship with our Creator so as to communicate with him and reflect his character. No other part of God's creation was given this privilege.

We were also made to share in the community of the one God who forever exists in three Persons: Father, Son, and Spirit. This is why God said, "Let us make people in our image" (notice the plurals). Community is critical for living well with God and with each other. It's what we're made to experience and enjoy.

In addition, women and men were called together to rule over the rest of the earth and its creatures. Leadership in the newly created world was given, from the start, to men and women as partners. God blessed them (again, it's plural) saying, "Be masters over all the animals." Though we were made differently from each other, we were intended to share this unique privilege and responsibility together.

After he had fashioned the first couple, "God saw all that he had made, and it was very good" (Gen. 1:31). What was good? Three things: (1) we were made in God's image, (2) we were created as male and female, and (3) we are to rule together over the rest of creation. The Bible's first words about gender relations are concise, almost cryptic. But, their message of mutuality and community is profound. It was meant to be a relationship between two different persons, which benefited both and harmed neither. With their beneficial differences they could work together to fulfill God's purposes in the new world.

The creation account that follows in chapter two provides considerably more detail about how God created us as men and women and, more importantly, why.

## *Why did God make us male and female?*

God first made a man from the ground and gave him life. But it was not good for him to remain alone; he needed a partner to help him. So, God fashioned a woman for him from his body. Adam called her Eve, because all human beings would come from her. This is how marriage began (Gen. 2:7, 18, 22–24; 3:20).

When I first started teaching in 1976 I made handouts with an old mimeograph machine. I mean the one with a big metal drum, waxy stencils, and nail polish to correct the mistakes made by typewriters. I know, some of you are saying, "What's a typewriter?" Or, I'd use carbon copy paper that was attached to an original standard paper sheet. These connected to ditto machines for copying and were less messy. Either method resulted in copies that were of inferior quality, often difficult to read. The copies did not reflect clearly the original from which they were taken.

Some understand the creation of the woman from the man in this way: the man was the perfect original; the woman was the inferior copy. Others point out that the animals came first; then God created Adam; then (drum roll please), the crowning achievement of the whole creation event was Eve. Neither is exactly the way the Bible tells the story.

As we look more closely at "Act Two" of the creation story, consider these questions. Why did the Creator design people as men and women? And, why did he fashion the first woman from the first man, instead of creating them both from the ground? The answers lie in the story itself.

God first created the man alone and allowed him to observe all the other creatures with their mates. In this way he would recognize that as a human he was alone, without a companion to share God's gracious gift of life. Moreover, he would have no one to help him in times of need, or to join with him in having children so that humanity could endure. The man by himself was unable to fulfill God's command to reproduce, and to fill and rule the earth (Gen. 1:28).

What does it mean when it says that the woman was made to be "a helper corresponding to" the man (Gen. 2:20; literal translation)? As a child, when I first read this story in the old King James Version, I thought "help meet" (KJV, ASV) must mean something like the boss's secretary, or perhaps a little girl who was allowed to "help" Mommy in the kitchen. In other words, her help was of lesser quality than the one she was helping.

However, in my journey of discovery, I found out that the original Hebrew term simply meant anyone who assisted another who was in need, regardless of which one of them might have been stronger or smarter than the other. In fact, most references in the Bible name God as the "helper." For example, God "helps Joseph" (Gen. 49:25) and is a "shield of help" for Israel (Deut. 33:29). The psalmist cries out in his need, "O Lord, be my helper" (Ps. 30:10), and the prophet Isaiah promises Israel that the Lord will "help" them (Isa. 41:10). Similarly, Abraham's trusted servant is named Eliezer ("my God is a helper"; Gen. 15:2) and Samuel sets up the monument Ebenezer ("stone of help") declaring, "Thus far the Lord has helped us" (1 Sam. 7:12). The list could go on.

Adam desperately needed the kind of help the animals could not give. Eve was uniquely designed to meet that need. As God often delivered Israel, Eve was to rescue Adam from his aloneness. But, unlike God, who was infinitely superior to Israel, she would be "a helper corresponding" to Adam, that is, a human being like him, neither superior nor subordinate. She would correspond to him as his companion and partner, so that as they shared life together they could help each other.

God fashioned the woman from the side of the man while he slept. I've often heard pastors say at weddings, "Eve was not taken from Adam's head to be superior to him, nor from his feet to be subordinate to him — rather, she was taken from his side to be his partner." I can't sum it up in a better way.

Have you ever watched the eyes of a groom, standing at the front of the church, when he sees his beautiful bride in her wedding gown for the first time? He looks like a little boy at Christmas. Yet, with Adam it was far more amazing! When he first witnessed what God had done for him he was stunned. "At last, my own flesh and bone!" he shouted. "I'll call her 'woman' because she was taken from man" (Gen. 2:23). Adam immediately recognized that she was a person, a human being like him, yet at the same time she was delightfully different — a perfect complement!

Speaking of weddings, Genesis 2 also explains the origin of a long established custom. The narrator comments, "This is why a man leaves his father and mother to unite with his wife" (Gen. 2:24).

Eve was taken from Adam and therefore should reunite with him — from "one flesh" to "one flesh." There was to be both diversity and unity. But there is also balance, for just as she was taken from him, so all human beings thereafter will come from her (Gen. 3:20). As there was an "order of creation," so there is an "order of procreation."

Paul Stookey, of Peter, Paul and Mary fame, set this idea to music in his well known 1971 "Wedding Song":

> A man shall leave his mother and a woman leave her home
> And they shall travel on to where the two shall be as one.
> As it was in the beginning is now and 'til the end
> Woman draws her life from man and gives it back again.
> And there is love. There is love.

Certainly, God could have created man and woman at the same time, separately from the ground. But this would not have illustrated nearly as well the beautiful, biblical truth of unity with diversity. Instead, they started as one and returned to being one again.

A former pastor and dear friend, Betty Coble-Lawther, showed an exercise to my wife Pat and me at a marriage seminar years ago. She had us take two pieces of construction paper (different colors) and glue them together. Then, after the glue dried, she asked us to try to separate them. This helped us to visualize what God means by the two becoming inseparably one.

Another way to look at the nature of this union is to consider the way electronic images are reproduced today. These can be copied as many times as we wish without losing any of the quality of the original. In fact, unless we choose to alter it in some way, the second image will have exactly the same quality as the original. So it is with God's creation of men and women. The emphasis is on what they shared in common. The woman was created as a human being corresponding to the man. They complemented each other in that they were slightly different, yet they shared God's image equally. The creative hand of God designed both him and her so they could reunite and become one in love and procreation. The privilege of Adam being the source of Eve's formation is balanced by the privilege of Eve being the source of all humanity to follow.

As I am writing, Pat is helping to care for our new twin granddaughters, Heidi and Kristen, along with their older brothers, Matthew and Zachary. Some day one of them may ask us, "Why did God make boys and girls different?" What should we tell them? We could tell them that God didn't want us to be alone, so he made two of us so that we could help each other. We could say that God loves unity between people, but also delights in wonderful diversity—and that only by working together can we fulfill God's purposes for humanity. We can assure them that being made either a boy or girl is a very good thing, for both genders reflect God's image.

I wish we could stop there. But, in order to be fully honest with our grandchildren, we must go on to tell them that the harmonious relationship for which we were created has been seriously damaged by our failure to do God's will. This is where Genesis 3 leads us down an old garden path.

## *What happened in the Garden of Eden?*

Eve ate the forbidden fruit, as did Adam, and God punished them both. God said to Eve, "In painful struggle you will bear children. You will desire your husband, though he will rule you." Then, God told Adam, "In painful struggle you will make a living from the ground — and then you will die" (Gen. 3:1–6, 14–20).

Some of you may be wondering at this point why I'm writing about sin and failure in a chapter titled "Discovering God's Good Creation". Well, there are two reasons. First, the beauty of the mutual partnership for which we were made stands out in clearer relief when set against the power struggles that resulted from humanity's failure. This is the interpretive context Scripture gives us. Second, it is the first time patriarchy (that is, "male rulership") appears in the Bible. The creation stories do not even allude to it!

We in the United States live in a competitive culture. It's drilled into us in our earliest experiences from school sports to grading curves and everything in between. On the positive side it can drive us to greater achievements in many different fields. On the negative side it can alienate us from each other, promoting a destructive win-at-any-cost mentality. Where did this all begin? You guessed it — right here in Genesis!

The scene opens with the adversary Satan appearing as a serpent so as to deceive the woman by challenging God's authority and integrity. Earlier, God told Adam that he should not eat from the tree of the knowledge of good and evil, and apparently, Adam passed that information on to Eve (Gen. 2:16–17). Yet, she was tricked into doing just that, after which Adam joined her and together the couple broke God's commandment.

Sadly, when God confronted them, neither was willing to take responsibility for their actions — instead they played the "blame game."

First, Adam blamed Eve as the woman whom God had given him. In other words, he was blaming God for giving him his companion. Then, Eve blamed the serpent, probably with the same implication regarding God. In the end, God judged each of them, but in reverse order: the serpent, the woman, and the man. So as to maintain balance, God confronts the man first, but judges the woman first. Neither is treated with privilege or prejudice. Rather, each is held responsible, though in different ways.

It is worth noting here that humanity will share in one aspect of the serpent's curse. A descendant of the woman will one day defeat the one represented by the serpent (Gen. 3:15). Though the woman must pay for her failure, there is grace in the judgment, for just as the woman led in the fall of humanity so she will lead in humanity's redemption! Jesus the Messiah will someday be "born of a woman" (Gal 4:4) with the purpose of redeeming humanity in his crucifixion and resurrection. As God had balanced the order of creation with that of procreation, and the order of confrontation with that of judgment, so he balances Eve's individual judgment with Mary's great privilege as the mother of Jesus.

It is also important to understand that the judgments (not curses) on the woman and the man are *descriptive* of what will come, not *prescriptive* of God's good intention in creation. In fact, they are a sad distortion of the creation model. The woman will bear children in painful struggle, and though her desire will be toward her husband, he will become her master (Gen. 3:16). Again, the key to understanding these words is their context. This is a judgment on humanity, not a blessing. God tells Eve how things will be from now on because of her sin. She will not only face a painful struggle in bearing children, but also a power struggle with her husband. She will desire to master him, but he will ultimately master her (compare the similar wording in the Cain and Able story in Gen. 4:7).

The judgment on Adam is similar to Eve's. He also faces a painful struggle, though his will be with the soil from which he was taken, and to which both of them will return. Each shares in the other's judgment, yet each has his and her different burden to bear. As a writer-speaker friend of ours, Jonalyn Grace Fincher, points out in her excellent book *Ruby Slippers*, "Men are not from Mars, nor are women from Venus — truth be told, we're both from Eden!"

It is important to realize that the power struggle between men and women — in which the man will emerge a ruler — appears first in the context of the painful struggles of Eve's childbearing and Adam's working the thorn-infested soil. As judgments for sin, both stand in contrast to God's original, good intention for humanity. In fact, Jesus came to redeem us from these things, to save us from the consequences of our failures. The great eighteenth century hymn writer Isaac Watts captured this message well in the familiar Christmas carol "Joy to the World":

No more let sins and sorrows grow,
Nor thorns infest the ground;
He comes to make His blessings flow
Far as the curse is found.

When we read Genesis 1–3 on its own terms, we are able to discover God's good creation in stark contrast to the marred relationships that resulted from our human failure. We also may realize how much of our own baggage we've been bringing with us, or how many of our own prejudices we have learned from family and culture.

It can be liberating to encounter the first couple in the beauty and simplicity of their mutual companionship. Their model is applicable whether you are married or single. The goal is to practice our mutual partnership as people created in God's image, whether spouses, brothers and sisters, or just friends.

The creation and fall story of Genesis 1–3 is primarily about the personal intimacy of the first man and woman, as well as their struggle together with human failure. Yet, the principles found here still apply to the way women and men relate today, both within and outside of marriage. However, care must be taken when making generalizations from the creation and fall texts. Our widely different experiences as individuals add a significant layer of complexity to the experience of just one man and one woman at the beginning of time. Keep this in mind as you reflect on these discussion questions.

## Reflection and Discussion

1. If you are married, what are two or three beneficial differences between you and your spouse? How can these be used to foster unity and harmony?

2. As an individual (single or married), what are some of the unique characteristics you possess that can benefit others in your life?

3. What are some examples of "corresponding helpers" in your experiences? Be specific.

4. Have you ever feared being alone, perhaps when separated from home or family? When has someone else been a helper to you at such a time?

5. Have there been times when you could have been a helper to another who was alone, but chose not to? What held you back from doing this?

6. Think about a time when you've been caught in a power struggle with a friend or spouse. Were you able to rise above the situation and restore mutuality? How were you able to do this?

7. When have power struggles ended badly for you? Is it too late to restore the relationship(s)? What might you do differently next time?

# — 2 —

# Learning from the Women of Scripture
*Biblical Narratives*

Everyone loves a good story. Storytelling touches our lives in ways that other teaching methods cannot. Jesus taught this way most of the time. When I speak with my students about the gender question, I often do the same.

In addition to the more commonly referenced passages, such as the ones discussed in the chapters that follow, I often point them to the stories of women in Scripture who have served in significant leadership roles, or to those who merely wish to sit at Jesus' feet and study as one of his disciples.

In this chapter, we will look at three such examples. Deborah was an Old Testament woman of strong character who led Israel by communicating the will of God to them through authoritative prophecy and judicial rulings. In the Gospels, Mary of Bethany provides a beautiful picture of a woman who was a disciple of Jesus. He openly commended her for choosing this path, though it went against the norms of the culture of that day. And finally, in Paul's greetings to the church at Rome he praises a woman named Junia, a co-worker of his who was outstanding among the apostles. All were extraordinary women used by God in extraordinary ways.

## *Does God speak or lead through women in the Bible?*

As a judge, Deborah held court on the main crossroads of Israel's hill country where people came to her to have their cases settled. As a prophet, she summoned Barak and ordered him on behalf of God to fight the Canaanites in the Jezreel Valley (Judg. 4:4–6).

No doubt, the most famous woman leader in Scripture is Deborah, empowered by God as both a prophet and judge to lead Israel at a critical time in its history. Her story in Judges 4–5 takes place at a time when there was no king in Israel and everyone did whatever seemed right to them (Judg. 17:6; 25:1). Even the great heroes of faith, like the judges Gideon, Barak, Samson, and Jephthah (Heb. 11:32–34), struggled in their relationship with God and their leadership of the young nation. Deborah stands out against this backdrop as a leader who served with excellence, as one who was respected and sought after by those she served.

A variety of images come to mind when we think of modern-day judges—usually coming from television courtroom dramas. But, what did it mean to be a judge in ancient Israel? Those judges served in two ways: settling civil disputes and leading armies into battle. In both capacities they spoke with authority, and their civil judgments and military orders were binding.

Deborah served as a judge primarily in the first sense, that of settling civil disputes. She held court under a palm tree named after her on the central crossroads of the country. Here people from all over the tribal territories could come to seek her wise judgment. She was well known and well respected for this administrative aspect of her job (Judg. 4:5). Judges like Deborah had the responsibility to discern truth while promoting unity among God's people. It was not an either-or choice! Rather, these two components made up the administrative side of a judge's duty. This was where her wisdom was translated into action.

But ancient judges, unlike contemporary judges, were also expected to lead their nation's armies into battle. Although Deborah could have tried to serve in this capacity too, she called a man from a tribal territory more than fifty miles away (a two-day journey by foot back then). Why? Again, her wisdom is evident. Apart from the fact that men generally are more skilled and experienced as warriors, Barak would have been familiar with the battlefield since it was close to his home. Good leaders choose good helpers to assist them in times of need.

In this context Deborah functioned as a prophet who spoke for God to God's people. Prophesying was similar to rendering judicial rulings because they both involved exercising authority on behalf of God.

To be clear, a prophet's authority was never intended by God to be found in the prophet himself or herself. Rather, they spoke with authority only when they accurately represented what God was saying. Nevertheless, they did speak with authority! For example, Deborah does not ask Barak politely what he thinks of leading an army into battle. No, she says, "The Lord, the God of Israel, commands you, 'Go, take 10,000 troops...and lead them up Mt. Tabor!'" (Judg. 4:6). She was his "commander-in-chief."

Curiously, Barak insists that Deborah accompany him into the battle. As a student in seminary, I used to think of Barak as a trembling coward clinging to Deborah's apron strings. Then, one day I noticed that he was listed in the New Testament as a great person of faith, those "of whom the world was not worthy" (Heb. 11:38). Perhaps he wanted a prophet with him in case he needed to make an emergency field decision in the heat of battle, or perhaps it was because the nation already respected Deborah's leadership.

Either way, Barak's request is best interpreted as an example of his faith in God and his willingness to submit to the Word of God delivered through God's messenger Deborah. This is also evident when he agrees to go to war knowing credit for the victory will go to yet another woman, Jael (Judg. 4:9, 16-23). This is not the action of a coward, but that of a great warrior who is at the same time humble enough to respect his commander — even if she's a woman.

There is no hint in the story of Judges 4-5 that God in any way disapproved of Deborah's service as either a prophet or a judge. Nor do we find the people of Israel reluctant to accept her rulings or go with her into battle. Instead Deborah serves as a stellar example of an extraordinary woman serving in extraordinary ways with God's blessing and power upon her. Like the family of the "woman of strong character" in Proverbs 31, Deborah's husband Lappidoth and their children — as well as generations to follow — have good cause to rise up and call her blessed!

## *What does Jesus think about women as disciples?*

Mary of Bethany was listening to Jesus teach, when her sister Martha insisted that she help in the kitchen. Jesus responded, "You worry about too many things, Martha. Only a few are needed — in fact, only one. Mary has chosen the best, and it will not be taken from her" (Luke 10:38-42).

Many of us grew up learning of Jesus' disciples through the catchy little song, "There were twelve disciples; Jesus called to help him, Simon Peter, Andrew, James, his brother John..." Or, if you're a bit more sophisticated, Leonardo Da Vinci's exquisite 1498 painting "Last Supper" might come to mind, with the twelve male disciples of Jesus sharing a final Passover with their Master.

Either way, you probably thought of Jesus' disciples as men — yes, all men. Seldom do we think of the larger group of seventy-two disciples that were also sent out by Jesus (Luke 10:1-23), or the women disciples who traveled with him and supported his ministry financially out of their own means. Some of these women even met with the inner circle of "The Twelve" (Luke 8:1-3). Mary of Bethany was a disciple of the Master like many other wise and courageous women in her day.

Martha and Mary lived with their brother Lazarus in the little village of Bethany, adjacent to Jerusalem on the eastern slope of the Mount of Olives. As followers of Jesus they would provide a place for him to stay when he was in the area. One day, Martha was making the customary preparations for dinner while Jesus and his disciples were visiting. When she noticed that her younger sister Mary was not helping her with the work, Martha went looking for her and found her sitting with the other disciples learning from the Master.

Indignantly, Martha rebuked her impetuous little sister for neglecting her traditional role, expecting to hear an endorsement from Jesus. Instead, he insisted that Mary had made the better choice. She dared to move beyond the limitations imposed by her culture and to join the disciples in learning from the greatest rabbi Israel had ever known. For this Jesus commends her, assuring her that she was welcome to share such a privileged place alongside the men.

There was only one thing really necessary for a first-century Jewish girl in Roman Palestine. No, it was not to cook and clean, or to be a good wife and give her husband children. These certainly would have ranked in the "few" important things, but not in the "one" thing that was necessary. The best thing Mary could do was to become a disciple of Jesus.

While I was in the midst of graduate study at Talbot in the mid-1970s, the school was just beginning to allow women to enroll in the Master of Divinity and Master of Theology programs. Though it had been founded in 1952, it took twenty-five years for its leadership to discover that it was okay for women to study the Bible and Christian theology at this level. It looked like a scene out of Barbara Streisand's 1983 film *Yentel!* Though we've come a long way since the young Jewish girl's 1904 Eastern Europe setting, many men and women in today's church still believe that such study belongs to men only.

Yet, an increasing number of women are now studying Scripture for themselves, and more specifically the gender question. Many of them simply want to know God's Word better by taking advantage of the numerous study tools previously made available only to men. Others are experiencing a clear call to professional ministry.

Several have shared with me their journeys, telling me of a "Martha" they knew — that is, a friend, relative, or sweetheart, who has told them to return to a more traditional role for women. "After all," they were told, "men's brains were designed by God to understand the Bible and theology better than women's." Or, as another colleague of mine put it, "Men sacrifice relationships for truth, while women sacrifice truth for relationships." Truth be told, both are sad and unfounded stereotypes that put stumbling blocks in the path of women called by God to ministry.

In contrast, it has been my privilege to tell such contemporary "Marys" that while remaining sensitive to the advice of others, they should follow the Master wholeheartedly as one of his disciples. In the words of Jesus, "only a few things are needed — in fact, only one."

## What does Paul think about women as apostles?

> Give my greetings to Andronicus and Junia, my Jewish kinfolk who were imprisoned with me. They are outstanding among the apostles, and believed in Jesus before I did (Rom. 16:7).

We often don't realize how preconceived ideas can affect the way we read a passage of Scripture, even though we really know better when we think about it. For example, when I first began to study the gender question, I assumed that only men could have been apostles in the Bible. After all, Jesus only let men be members of the select group of "The Twelve." In addition, this assumption seemed consistent with what I read in my New American Standard Bible, which had the man's name "Junias" in Romans 16:7 instead of the woman's name "Junia" (as in my paraphrase above, as well many other versions). What's going on here?

Let's start with the question, "Why did Jesus select twelve Jewish men as his most intimate group of disciples?" Yes, the "Jewish" part got left out of the little song we learned. But to be thorough, we need to consider why there were "twelve" and why they were all "Jewish" in addition to why they were all "men." When all these facts are taken together the answer becomes clear. Though the gospel was intended to eventually reach all ethnic groups, it was preached first to God's Old Covenant people, the Jews (Paul's writing reflects this in Rom. 1:16; 2:9–10). With this in mind, the number twelve could easily have represented the twelve tribes of Israel, and Jewish men would have completed the symbolism of traditional Jewish leadership. In other words, in addition to the convenience of having the same gender travel together in a small and intimate group (significant in itself), Jesus used the model of "twelve Jewish men" to be a good witness to the Jewish audience he was seeking to reach first.

However, this doesn't mean we take a quantum leap to insist that women and Gentiles be excluded from church leadership (oddly enough, people often assume that women should be excluded and Gentiles should be included)! If we are going to restrict women today because women were not among "The Twelve," then we should allow only Jewish believers to lead the church and require elder boards to have twelve members. But this isn't the point the biblical writers are making. Rather, Paul moved the Galatians beyond the strictly Jewish model in order to embrace a growing Gentile congregation (as we will discover in chapter three). In fact, Paul explicitly applies the same principle to women (Gal. 3:28).

Now, what about "Junia" vs. "Junias" in Paul's greetings to the church at Rome (Rom. 16:7)? Well, when I looked more deeply into this question years ago, I discovered that the feminine "Junia" in more recent translations is not the result of the modern women's movements of the nineteenth–twentieth centuries. This is clear from the fact that as early as 1611 the "authorized" King James Version rendered the feminine "Junia." However, some versions appearing in the twentieth century (for example, ASV, NASB) changed this to the masculine "Junias." Why?

Again, I dug deeper and found that the majority of Greek manuscripts read "Iounian," which could be translated with the feminine "Junia" or the masculine "Junias." A few Greek manuscripts read "Julia" (another woman's name). So, how does one decide? The fact is there are many examples of the woman's name "Junia" in Greek literature during this time, while there is no example of the man's name "Junias." Given this, and the alternate manuscript reading of "Julia," it seems far more likely this is a woman's name. Fortunately, more recent translations like the New International Version and the New Living Translation have returned to this earlier and more accurate translation.

What then does Paul say about the woman Junia? He declares that she and Andronicus are "outstanding among the apostles." Junia is not just an apostle; she's an outstanding apostle! And, what did she do as an "apostle"? The word means, literally, "one sent out" with the gospel message. They were like modern day evangelists and missionaries except that, in the formative days of the early church, apostles carried more authority. People in the church then did not yet have copies of the Scripture to read — especially the New Testament. So, apostles delivered correct doctrine to the people, much like Priscilla and Aquila (a husband and wife team) did with Apollos in Acts 18:24–26. Moreover, they did so with "apostolic authority," as Paul himself often emphasizes in his letters (Rom. 1:1; 1 Cor. 1:1; 2 Cor. 1:1; Gal. 1:1).

In sum, the stories of Deborah, Mary, and Junia are representative of other women in the Bible, such as the prophets Miriam (Micah 6:4; Exod. 15:20), Huldah (2 Kings 22:8–20; 2 Chron. 34:19–28) and Anna (Luke 2:36–38), as well as the disciples Joanna (the manager of Herod's household), Mary Magdalene, and Susanna, who sometimes even traveled with The Twelve (Luke 8:1–3). Yes, courageous women were called to challenge traditional assumptions about gender roles throughout Scripture. Thankfully, many responded to God's leading to study, teach, and give leadership to God's people alongside their brothers.

## Reflection and Discussion

1. Have you ever heard or told a "story of struggle" that a woman endured in her journey because of gender? What caused it? What lessons can be learned?

2. Is there a "Deborah" among you that speaks God's Word with great courage (a preacher), or has gifts and wisdom in administration (a deacon or elder)? What could you and your church do as a "Barak" to encourage her?

3. What concrete steps could your church take to better encourage a "Mary" among you that wishes to pursue deeper discipleship training and education in the Bible and theology?

4. If you are a woman, can you name any men in your life that have encouraged you in discipleship or ministry? What meant the most? If you are a man, have you ever served as Jesus' voice of endorsement to a "Mary" in your life?

5. Is there a "Junia" in your congregation—a missionary, evangelist, or teacher—who is "outstanding" in what she does? If so, is there a "Paul" among you who endorses her work publicly?

6. Have you ever invoked a church tradition or cultural norm in order to "put a woman back in her place"? Or, are you a woman who has experienced this? How can the stories of these biblical women serve as a corrective to such abuses?

— 3 —

# Embracing our Oneness in Christian Community
*Galatians 3*

> As believers we are all children of God through faith, regardless of ethnicity, social status, or gender. These old divisions are no longer relevant in Christ's church. Instead, we are to live as a unified community of co-heirs to God's promises (Gal. 3:26–28).

Think about the church where you worship or about a Christian organization with which you are familiar. Do the issues of ethnicity, social status, or gender still pose a problem? How about with you personally? Are you having trouble sorting out preconceived ideas and assumptions from biblical truth? How should we as Christians respond to the changes that have come over the past century or two? Does it sometimes all just feel overwhelming?

Take courage, our God is a God of hope! The mutual partnership that Adam and Eve lost in Eden can still be restored in genuine Christian community. If fact, that's God's plan! In the community of the church, God addresses the seemingly insurmountable problem of the "painful struggle" between women and men that arose because of sin. Here Eve's promised descendant (Jesus) has crushed the head of the serpent in the redemptive event of the cross (Gen. 3:15; Gal. 4:4). A new era has dawned.

Nowhere are the ramifications of this wonderful truth for gender relationships presented more clearly and directly than in Paul's letter to the churches in the Roman province of Galatia (now central Turkey). Written early in his ministry (around 48–55 AD), Galatians is dedicated almost entirely to the problem of unity between Jewish and non-Jewish (or "Gentile") believers. In response to the divisions between them, the apostle boldly proclaims, "There is neither Jew nor Gentile, neither slave nor free — there is not male and female — for you are all one in Jesus the Messiah" (Gal. 3:28).

Paul's unusually strong and unqualified proclamation here is striking, especially if you consider his background. Paul was a conservative Jewish rabbi and a Roman citizen who came to faith in Jesus as the Messiah. As a learned man in the Greco-Roman world, he might have been familiar with Socrates' praise to the pagan gods for being born a human instead of an animal, a man instead of a woman, and a Greek instead of another ethnicity. As a Jewish rabbi, he almost certainly knew the classical Talmudic prayer, "Thank God that I'm not a slave, Gentile, or woman!"

This may be why Paul broadens the scope of his statement to include slaves and women. But what was the point he was making about Gentiles to begin with? The key to understanding Paul's declaration can be found in Galatians, as well as in his short letter to a close friend and slave owner named Philemon.

## What do Jews and Gentiles have to do with the gender question?

Everything! Paul, a Jewish rabbi who was called by God to be an apostle to the Gentiles, gives his readers a paradigm for understanding how ethnicity, social status, and gender are to be addressed in the Christian church. In short, what Christ's death on the cross did for Gentiles, it also did for slaves and women in the new community of God's people.

In Galatians 1, Paul argues that the full gospel of justification by faith has been extended to Gentile believers through his ministry — which carries apostolic authority (1:1, 6–9, 13–19). In chapter 2, he makes it clear that Gentiles do not need to live as Jews in order to be fully included in God's New Covenant community, the church. For example, not even Titus, a Greek convert and co-laborer with Paul, was compelled to observe the Jewish practice of circumcision (2:1–5). On another occasion, Paul went so far as to publicly condemn the apostle Peter (imagine being present for that encounter), along with other Jewish believers, because they refused to sit at the table in fellowship with Gentile believers (2:11–14). One would have expected more from Peter after God led him to Cornelius' house to witness the powerful conversion of that Gentile family (Acts 10:1–48)!

When I first began studying the Book of Galatians, many of my Bible teachers told me that Paul was only concerned with how God forgives sin by grace alone — whether we are Jewish or not. They assured me that it didn't have much at all to do with how we lived as Christ's church after we became believers.

Another take on Paul's words came from our son Brett when he was in second grade at a Christian school. His teacher required the students to memorize several key Bible verses that included Galatians 3:28. While I was driving Brett to school one morning, we were reviewing his memory verse for the week. Since he already knew it fairly well, I decided to ask him what he thought it meant (teachers do that sort of thing). To my surprise he replied without hesitation, "Oh our teacher already told us that. It means that someday we'll all be equal in heaven."

Do Paul's words really apply only to the initial stage of becoming believers or to how we will someday relate in heaven? A closer look at the book of Galatians will reveal something quite different.

Think about it for a minute. If the apostle were only concerned with how people initially came to faith in Jesus, why then does he use examples of circumcision, holiday observance, and table-fellowship regarding Gentiles who are already believers? After all, Gentiles have been coming to faith at least since a Canaanite prostitute named Rahab helped Joshua in the conquest of the land (Josh. 2:1–21; 6:15–25) and a Moabite woman named Ruth married the Judean Boaz (Ruth 1-4). In fact, both of these Gentile women are listed as ancestors of Jesus the "Jewish" Messiah (Matt. 1:5; Heb. 11:31; Jam. 2:25)!

Rather, the issue at hand for Paul in Galatians is how we live together as God's people after we've come to believe that Jesus is the Messiah. Can Gentile believers ignore the old Jewish customs and still be members in good standing of the church? After all, the Law of Moses commands these customs.

Paul's answer is straightforward and practical. He declares that we have all become Christians through faith by God's grace — both Jews and non-Jews. Moreover, the Law of Moses has now been replaced by the gospel of grace to all who believe, not just Jews. All Christians are united in Jesus the Messiah. Paul's emphasis to the Galatians is, "You've become one by believing, now live that way with the Gentiles — indeed, even with slaves and women!"

## What does it mean to be "one in Jesus the Messiah"?

Circumcision is quite common for newborn boys in the modern era. And it is not always associated with Jewish people. However, the custom is ancient, and at one time was specifically designated by God as a sign of being his chosen people.

The community of believers in the New Covenant that Jesus established with the church is fundamentally different from that of the Old Covenant with the nation of Israel. Under the old arrangement, God used the Hebrew people (later known as Israel, then as the Jews) to bring his message to the world. All who were associated with the Israelite model of community had to circumcise their children as a sign of their commitment to this arrangement (Gen. 17:1–14).

When Israel became a nation, its people were not supposed to associate with the non-Israelites who lived around them and practiced pagan religions. These "Gentiles" could join Israel by acknowledging the one true God, but they had to be circumcised along with their children and forsake their pagan practices. This allowed them to live among the Israelites, though not with full citizenship rights.

The "Jew and Gentile" distinction remained throughout Old Testament history. Gentiles could become believers who were fully equal in their spiritual standing before God, but they could not fully live out that status with Israelite members of the Old Covenant community. Circumcision was required of Gentile believers, yet they could not always "sit at the table" with Jewish believers.

When God made all believers one in Jesus, a radical change took place. Under the New Covenant model (Luke 22:25; 2 Cor. 3:6), circumcision was replaced by the "new creation" where all believers are reconciled to God and to each other through a spiritual rebirth (2 Cor. 5:16–21; John 3:1-14). The old model was reversed so that circumcision was no longer required and so that everyone in the new community of faith enjoyed full citizenship. The Jewish "Messiah" (meaning "Anointed One") was also anointed to be the Redeemer of Gentiles.

At the heart of Paul's argument in Galatians is a unified community where the old divisive barriers of lifestyle (not salvation) are broken down. Addressing this same problem in his letter to the believers at Ephesus, Paul tells them that Jesus has united Jews and Gentiles by destroying the dividing wall of hostility between them with the purpose of fusing the two groups into one new humanity that will be known as his body, the church (Eph. 2:14–15).

So what's the bottom line? All believers in Jesus now have full citizenship in the church — with all of its rights and privileges! The old barriers are gone.

## *Is there a place at the table for slaves and women?*

Paul once said to Philemon, a dear friend and partner in Christian service, "Stop treating your slave Onesimus like a slave. Instead, treat him like your brother in the Lord, because that's what he really is" (Philem. 17–21).

In addition to Gentiles, two other groups were also among those with "second-class citizenship" under the Old Covenant: slaves and women. Slaves were normally disadvantaged Gentiles and were thus usually treated with the same exclusions as other Gentiles—only worse. And, women—even Israelite women—were restricted from certain aspects of worship and service at the Tabernacle, even if they were descendants of Levi. Neither slaves nor women enjoyed the full citizenship rights of Israelite free men.

So what does Paul's letter to Philemon have to say about this? This letter is focused entirely on the slavery question—specifically a runaway slave by the name of Onesimus—just as Galatians was focused almost entirely on the Gentile question. Though Paul's letter was in the form of a personal note to his friend Philemon, it was also to be shared with the local believers that met in Philemon's home in a town not far from the province of Galatia.

Under Roman law, a runaway slave faced death by his owner if caught. This makes Paul's "request" of Philemon, sent by the hand of Onesimus himself, even more extraordinary. With the church in his home as witness, Paul calls Philemon to treat Onesimus no longer as a slave, but as a dear brother in the Lord (Philem. 16). The apostle overrides the old division between slaves and masters by calling for a new relationship between two brothers in Christ. More specifically, he instructs the one with power to relinquish it for the sake of the other, as well as for the sake of the gospel. The reason was that God had established a new model of community that included both Gentiles and slaves as full partners with Jewish free men.

You might be thinking right now, "What's so new about all of this? The church is practically all Gentile today." But, stop and think of how very recently we've recognized that slaves and free should be one community, both in the church and the broader society. I was a teenager growing up in the Philadelphia area in 1963 when Dr. Martin Luther King, Jr. gave his unforgettable speech, "I Have a Dream," I went to college in Arkansas (1965-69) in a town where African Americans were not permitted food or lodging. And now we have witnessed the election of Barack Obama as the first African American president of the United States.

Yes, I know that racial slavery is in some ways different from the economic slavery that Paul addressed. Nevertheless, in the end both kinds of slavery exclude a certain group of people from being fully functioning members of a community. It took the church a very long time to recognize our error regarding slavery, though for all practical purposes we've finally made it to that place. Regretfully, we're not quite there yet regarding gender.

So this is where the question of gender enters into the picture. Put in the same category as Gentiles and slaves, women were generally excluded from "sitting at the table" with men in Paul's day. Like Mary of Bethany, they were expected to be serving in the kitchen rather than discussing more important matters with Jesus and the disciples. But Paul declared that the truth of the gospel changes all of that. In fact, by altering the grammatical structure slightly, Paul emphasizes most strongly the "not male or female" part of Galatians 3:28. It is like saying, "Yes, even women are welcome at the table!"

With such a clear statement as this, why are the issues of ethnicity, social status, and gender still a problem in today's churches—especially gender? Many churches today are still reluctant to embrace their oneness in Christ by welcoming women to the table of fellowship along with men. Some would say that later in Paul's writings he makes some restrictive comments regarding women that significantly qualify his statement here in Galatians. We'll see if that is actually the case when we examine these passages in the chapters that follow. When I first did that, I was surprised at what I found—and even more so at what I did not find.

But for now, can we acknowledge that Paul in his letter to the Galatians does not qualify his inclusion of women as fully functioning members of the New Covenant community? Gentiles and slaves are welcomed in today's churches at all levels of participation without restriction—why not women?

## Reflection and Discussion

1. The issue of privilege or discrimination based on ethnic background is still a problem in many churches. What can your church do better to remove such barriers? Are you willing to get involved?

2. Can you remember (or can you consider) April 4, 1968 when Martin Luther King, Jr. was assassinated? How has your attitude (or how have attitudes in general) toward racial discrimination changed since then? What brought about that change?

3. Slavery in the Bible was mostly about social status (not ethnicity). How does the issue of social status play itself out in your church or at your work? What is one step you can take to bring positive change?

4. When Paul made his remarkable statement in Galatians 3:28, he did not qualify it. Why are we often so quick to qualify this otherwise inclusive statement regarding half of the church?

5. Certainly it was hard for Philemon to get over his "history" with his slave Onesimus (and vice versa). What baggage do you bring that makes you reluctant to affirm women as equals in the Christian community? How can you get past it?

6. Do you believe that other passages in the Bible stand in tension with or qualify Galatians 3:28? If so, which ones, and how do they do so? Try to be specific.

# Principles for Today

You've just experienced a high-speed journey through biblical history, from God's good creation of all things at the beginning of the Old Testament to Jesus' great redemptive act of love in the New Testament. Let's review what we've discovered, and then apply the principles we've learned to our lives as Christians.

In chapter one, we learned that God created humanity in the divine image as male and female and called us to rule the world together. The creative design and mandate reveal a shared partnership between people who are alike, though each possesses beneficial differences (Gen. 1). The example of Adam and Eve as corresponding helpers, the balanced orders of creation and procreation, and the reuniting of two who had been separated in creation (Gen. 2), all reinforce this understanding of the design. Taken together, the creation accounts paint a beautiful portrait of mutuality untainted by the dominance of patriarchy.

Tragically, the relationship of the first couple was marred by their failure to live in harmony with each other and with God (Gen. 3). Because of this, they would experience painful toil in their individual lives and a power struggle with each other. In the end, patriarchy would replace mutual partnership as a sad distortion of God's good intention for humankind. Only the promise that the descendant of Eve would someday crush the Serpent's head would sustain hope for redemption.

In chapter two, we examined the examples of three brave women in Scripture: Deborah, Mary, and Junia. These represent many other women in the biblical narrative who were risk-takers for God. Deborah gave courageous leadership to Israel during a dark and difficult era as a judge, prophet, and military commander (Judg. 4–5). Mary of Bethany was a dedicated disciple of Jesus Christ (Luke 10). Like many other women of her day she chose to follow the Master in the one thing that really matters. And, the great apostle Paul recognized Junia of Rome as one of the most outstanding apostles he knew (Rom. 16). She, along with many other godly Christian women, worked side by side with their brothers in Christ as leaders of the early church. Like the woman of wisdom in Proverbs 31, these women of strong character are given to us in Scripture to encourage today's women to dare to be all that God wants them to be.

In chapter three, we considered the radical change that took place with the coming of Jesus the Messiah and the formation of a new community of God's people, the church. In Christ, traditional barriers such as ethnicity (Jew above Gentile), social status (free person above slave) and gender (male above female) were rendered irrelevant for both faith and practice. Under the New Covenant, Christians are called to embrace their oneness by standing firm in this freedom. Indeed, we are to fully welcome all believers into our fellowship in both word and deed, without discrimination.

The Bible is God's Word to us, given so that we might live under its authority. This means we are obligated to discern the enduring principles that it teaches and apply them to our lives. So let's do just that.

First, the unity and diversity — that is, mutuality — of men and women that is so evident in creation provides a model for all human relationships. God designed us to live with each other as corresponding helpers, or partners. Though a married couple was used as the first model for this, the general principle of partnership is not limited to marriage. In all of our relationships, we must celebrate both our unity as human beings and our diversity as male and female. In fact, most partnerships are formed both because of what we share in common and because of what each individual can bring to the union.

Second, patriarchy first appeared in human history in God's words of judgment to Eve — yet its lingering effects are still with us. However, the good news is that Jesus came to deliver us from that judgment! We all agree that it's good to work toward a world that is free from painful struggles with something as simple as weeds in the garden or as significant as complications in childbirth. But, to be consistent, we should acknowledge that it is also good to work toward a world that replaces male dominance with mutual partnership.

Third, God has chosen, empowered, and blessed great women leaders in the Bible, who broke from the feminine stereotypes of their day in order to serve the God who called them. When we face difficult decisions in our churches today, will we actively invite the counsel of wise women like Deborah? And, when one like her addresses our congregation, will we respond in faith and obedience like Barak? When we recount the work of the great apostles of Scripture that laid the foundation for the church, will we honor Junia as Paul did? And, when we think of sending our best young people for graduate study in Bible and theology, will we fully affirm those women that wish to follow the Master like Mary of Bethany? We must answer these challenging questions in the affirmative. This is no time for evangelicals to remain silent!

Finally, Jesus Christ, the descendant of Eve that was promised in Genesis 3:16, has come—in fact, he came over 2,000 years ago! Moreover, his coming established the church, a new community of God's people in which the barriers of ethnicity, status, and gender were rendered irrelevant. Don't you think it's about time we embraced this precious gift of oneness in Christ more fully? This is a time to stand firm in the truth of the full gospel of grace, as well as in the freedom for which Christ has set us free. We must reach beyond patriarchy to partnership, beyond law to grace, even beyond Eden to a new creation! Let us celebrate in word and deed the goodness of God's creation design of mutuality, along with the lives of the godly women of Scripture who shared spiritual leadership with their brothers—indeed in the oneness of Christian community!

# PARTNERS
*in Marriage*

# — 4 —

# Yielding to Each Other in Love
### *1 Corinthians 7*

Be attentive to the sexual needs of your spouse — husbands and wives alike. Both of you should yield authority over your own bodies to the other. And, don't neglect each other except by mutual consent and in order to commit to a short time of prayer (1 Cor. 7:1-6).

Does fear hold us back from yielding our perceived sense of authority to our spouse? Sometimes the answer is "yes," and for good reason. Almost certainly you either have a sad story to tell, or know of someone who does, where yielding authority by one spouse resulted in the wielding of authority by the other. Perhaps some of you have chosen not to marry because of this fear.

Intimate relationships carry with them great risk. That's why, as the old saying has it, "Marriage ought not to be entered into lightly, or unadvisedly, but in the fear of the Lord."

No biblical text addresses the issue of mutual partnership in marriage in a more balanced and extensive way than 1 Corinthians 7:1-40. Yet, none has been more neglected in contemporary writings on the gender question. Let's try to help correct that error!

In this chapter, Paul answers a letter that the believers in Corinth had sent to him earlier. Though we don't know exactly what their questions were, we can still learn a lot from the apostle's answers. In his reply, Paul corrects the distorted view of marriage held by many in that church who believed they were living in the last days and therefore should abstain from marriage — or at least sex within marriage.

The thread that weaves all of the diverse issues in this chapter together is mutuality. Paul is careful to address men and women even-handedly in no less than twelve areas in this one chapter. This section is longer and more comprehensive than any other passage on marriage in Scripture — in fact, more so than all the biblical "gender texts" combined!

Before we discuss just a few of the issues Paul raises, notice the deliberate symmetry in his words regarding mutuality as it relates to marriage — or the choice not to marry. The list in the following chart is almost overwhelming.

### 1. Fidelity in Marriage (7:2)
Each man should be sexually intimate with his own wife, and each woman should be sexually intimate with her own husband.

### 2. Spousal Rights (7:3)
The husband should fulfill his marital duty to his wife; and likewise also, the wife to her husband.

### 3. Yielding of Authority (7:4)
The wife does not have authority over her own body but yields it to her husband. In the same way, the husband does not have authority over his own body but yields it to his wife.

### 4. Consent for Abstinence (7:5–6)
Do not deprive each other except perhaps by mutual consent and for a time, so that you may devote yourselves to prayer.

### 5. Loss of a Spouse to Death (7:8–9)
Now to the unmarried [widowers] and the widows I say: It is good

for them to stay unmarried, as I do. But if they cannot control themselves, they should marry.

### 6. Initiating Divorce with a Believer (7:10–11)

A wife must not separate from her husband (but if she does, she must remain unmarried or else be reconciled to her husband); and a husband must not divorce his wife.

### 7. Initiating Divorce with an Unbeliever (7:12–13)

If any brother has a wife who is not a believer and she is willing to live with him, he must not divorce her. And if a woman has a husband who is not a believer and he is willing to live with her, she must not divorce him.

### 8. Sanctification of an Unbelieving Spouse (7:14)

The unbelieving husband has been sanctified through his wife, and the unbelieving wife has been sanctified through her believing husband.

### 9. Responsibility when an Unbelieving Spouse Leaves (7:15)

But if the unbeliever leaves, let it be so. The brother or sister is not bound in such circumstances; God has called us to live in peace.

### 10. Salvation of an Unbelieving Spouse (7:16)

How do you know, wife, whether you will save your husband? Or, how do you know, husband, whether you will save your wife?

### 11. Change of Status (7:26–28a)

Because of the present crisis, I think that it is good for a man to remain as he is. Are you pledged to a woman? Do not seek to be released. Are you free from such a commitment? Do not look for a wife. But if you do marry, you have not sinned; and if a virgin marries, she has not sinned.

### 12. Devotion to Ministry (7:28b, 32, 34)

Those who marry will face many troubles in this life, and I want to spare you this…The unmarried man is focused on the Lord to please the Lord…The unmarried woman or virgin is focused on the Lord to be holy in body and spirit.

## *Which spouse has authority in a marriage?*

If you are married, how many times have you disagreed with your spouse over something related to sexual intimacy? Okay, you don't need to say it out loud. But, let's face it; this is a difficult reality in most marriages, even a cause for the failure of many. In any given marriage, one spouse is likely to have a stronger sex drive than the other. Moreover, this can reverse itself as time goes by for a number of reasons, creating a challenging mid-life transition for many couples.

Thankfully, the apostle Paul addresses sexual intimacy in marriage head-on in the first four of his twelve mutuality statements (7:2–5). Paul is concerned here that an individual's unfulfilled desire for sexual intimacy may lead to seeking a solution in an extra-marital affair. Although the term is not popular in contemporary society, the Bible calls this "immorality." Therefore, he encourages the one with a strong sex drive to find a suitable partner and marry, and the one already married to be sensitive to the sexual desire of his or her spouse.

Though Paul chose to remain single in order to devote himself more fully to the Lord's calling in his life, he allows other believers the freedom to fully enjoy God's gift of marriage. Moreover, he declares that in the most intimate aspect of being married, neither spouse should exercise authority over the other. Rather, each is to yield his or her authority to the one with whom they share God's gracious gift of life. Moreover, they should enjoy the pleasure of sexual intimacy in marriage often — yes, often — though it is not about either demanding his or her rights. In fact, to abstain from sex for extended periods of time — even for prayer — should only be done by mutual consent for a relatively short time.

I cannot overemphasize here the importance of Paul's words. This is the only place in the Bible where the word "authority" is used in connection with marriage. Yes, that's right, the only place! And here the point is that neither spouse has authority over his or her body; instead, each is to yield that right to the other. This is consistent with Paul's words to

Philemon regarding his slave Onesimus. The one who had the authority (in that case the slave-master) was told to let go of it — that is, stop treating the slave as a slave, but instead treat him as a brother (Philemon 16).

Furthermore, we will discover in the next chapter in this book that this was a pattern for Paul. He never calls Gentiles, slaves, or women to rise up and demand their rights. Instead, he calls Jews, masters, and men to let go of their presumed authority or privilege and treat Gentiles, slaves, and women as equal partners in the gospel. Are you listening, men? The example for Paul is Jesus himself:

> In your relationships with each other, have the same attitude Jesus had. Though he is equal with God, he freely let go of this advantage and became a mortal like us — even a humble servant willing to die for our sins (Phil. 2:5–8).

Sadly, one critically important caveat must be added. Whereas Paul calls both slaves and wives to submit, he never tells them to remain in an abusive relationship. Some would point out that Paul does not address this issue directly — that's true. However, in the context of the Bible's silence we should follow the gracious and compassionate example of Jesus toward those who were oppressed in the society of his day. In fact, the virtue of protecting marginalized and oppressed people groups is clearly taught in both the Old and New Testaments (for example, Job 31:16; Isa. 10:2; Zech. 7:10; James 1:27).

## What about separation and divorce?

About half of the marriages in western societies end in either separation or divorce — yes, even many Christian marriages. I grew up in an extended family where divorce was quite common. And, it's only by God's grace that my wife Pat and I were able to find our way through several years of deep struggle that could have easily led us down the same road. Like the wandering character "Pilgrim" in John Bunyan's *Pilgrim's Progress*, we know that in our marriage of over forty years we still must choose daily to "walk on the path" or suffer the tragic consequences.

But as mortals we do sometimes stray off the path. This is why divorce, while never encouraged in the Bible, is permitted — though only under the most severe circumstances. Let's look at the Old Testament and Gospels background first, then Paul's words to the Corinthians.

In Matthew 19:1-9, Jesus tells the religious leaders of his day that divorce was originally allowed by Moses because of the hardness of human hearts and that it should be permitted only in extreme cases like adultery (19:8). This echoes the declaration of the prophet Malachi that "God hates divorce" (Mal. 2:16). So the general principle is to avoid separation and divorce if at all possible.

The only other noteworthy exception is that of Ezra the scribe, who tells the Jews who had married unbelievers during the Babylonian captivity to divorce them (Ezra 10:11). Marrying "outside the faith" was a serious problem throughout Israel's history — the most famous example being Solomon whose pagan wives actually turned his heart away from following the one true God (1 Kings 11:1-6).

So, what does all of this have to do with 1 Corinthians 7:10-16? Here Paul gives a general rule stated in carefully balanced terms that men and women should not separate from or divorce their spouses (10-13). Even when the spouse is not yet a believer, Paul advises both women and men to "stay in the marriage" in order to be a positive influence on their spouses and children (14, 16).

However, the apostle then balances his instruction with words of grace, affirming that God desires peace in circumstances beyond our control (15). I firmly believe that the grace shown in this passage allows a woman suffering in a relationship with an abusive man (or vice versa) to take the necessary steps to bring peace to her life and the lives of their children — even if it means, as a last resort, separation or divorce.

That being said, don't miss the positive impact that a believing wife or husband can bring to his or her spouse by remaining in the marriage.

Either can be a "sanctifying influence" to the one who does not yet believe. In other words, the believer can provide an atmosphere of spiritual benefit for the unbeliever, as well as for their children. Moreover, Paul asks rhetorically, "Who knows, whether the unbeliever might eventually come to salvation" as a result of the witness of the believing partner.

It is significant that the decision to stay or leave, as well as the sanctifying or saving benefits of a believer, can work either way: from the husband to the wife, or from the wife to the husband. As always with Paul, the marriage relationship should be one of mutual partnership.

## Is it better to stay single?

In my high school days (early 1960s), we pretty much expected to get married shortly after graduation. Moreover, a man or woman who chose not to marry was viewed either with pity or suspicion. In distain we thought, "He will probably be a bachelor forever." Or, "She just might die an old maid." We might have even been tempted to presume some "matchmaking skills," along with the privilege to employ them. Except for priests and nuns, most people then did not view remaining single in a positive light.

Today, things are a bit different. People regularly delay marriage until they are "thirty-something" and have a career well established. Getting married or staying single are both considered valid options.

## What advice does the Bible give regarding this issue?

When Jesus gave his strict ruling on divorce (Matt. 19:10), his disciples responded, "Well then, I suppose it's better not to get married!" To their surprise, Jesus allowed for this option because he knew that some could not handle the commitment required for a lasting marriage (11–12). He said, in effect, "If you're not ready for the commitment, then don't make it!"

And, Paul goes even further by holding up singleness as a virtue. Throughout 1 Corinthians 7:1-40, he affirms its benefits. He begins by saying that it is good for a man or woman (clearly, in this context, one who was unmarried) not to be sexually active (1). In other words, remaining single is okay—in fact, it's good! Moreover, he goes on to express his personal preference that all of his readers would have the gift of celibacy as he does (6-7), advising those not yet committed to marriage to consider staying single (27). He explains that being single frees a man or woman for greater commitment to service for Christ and the church because they are not distracted with the obligations of marriage (32-35, 40).

Paul adds one caveat to this instruction. If someone who is single chooses to marry, it should be to another believer (39). He reinforces this in his second letter to the Corinthians by saying that believers should not be joined in marriage to unbelievers (2 Cor. 6:14) because of the temptation to fall away from the faith (14-18). No doubt he remembered Israel's tragic example during Ezra's time that we discussed earlier.

So in this chapter, Paul addresses the issues of authority in marriage, separation and divorce, singleness, and marriage to someone who is not yet a believer. And in every one of these areas he emphatically affirms an equal sense of mutuality between men and women—yes, twelve times in one chapter! The idea of gender equality inside and outside of marriage did not begin with the women's movements of the nineteenth-twentieth centuries. Rather, the apostle Paul preached this message nearly 2,000 years ago.

# Reflection and Discussion

1. If you are married—or in a relationship that's heading in that direction—how often have you argued over who should be in charge? How could you reshape such discussions so as to yield authority mutually instead of wielding it?

2. When you discuss the gender issue with someone, are you ever afraid to advocate equality and mutuality because of what someone might think? Why? Does Paul's affirmation of these ideals give you more confidence?

3. Is the experience of sexual intimacy in your marriage falling short of your expectations or your spouse's? What can you (not your spouse) do to better practice the biblical principle of "yielding rights"?

4. How has divorce impacted you and your church? What can you do to encourage others to consider this option only in the most extreme circumstances? How can you show greater compassion and forgiveness to others who have failed or suffered in this way?

5. If you are single, how have your friends and family reacted? How has this freed you to give more time to serve Christ and the church? What unique responsibilities come with singleness?

6. Though God created sexual intimacy for marriage, it has become popular today to be sexuality active before such a commitment is made. If this is true of you, are you willing to move beyond this and choose either abstinence or a faithful marriage commitment?

7. If you are married to a non-believer, how could you live better so as to lead him or her to faith? What could you do to help your children choose this path? If you are considering marriage, are you willing to share it only with another believer?

# — 5 —

# Loving and Serving Each Other
*Ephesians 5*

Be filled with God's Spirit, submitting to each other out of reverence for Christ—wives, to your own husbands as unto the Lord. Husbands love your wives as Christ, the head of his body the church, loved and died for her (Eph. 5:18, 21-33).

I can remember on many occasions hearing a minister say to a bride, "God wants you to submit to your husband, obeying him in all things." Then, he would turn to the groom and say, "And God wants you to be the spiritual leader of your wife and make the final decisions in your marriage when necessary. As head of the house, you are now responsible before God for both yourself and your wife."

Though there was some truth in the pastor's words, I discovered over time that he had embellished the biblical text a bit—in fact, quite a bit! Let's look together at the Ephesians text and see exactly what it does say—and what it does not!

## Does "mutual" mean what I think it does?

Ephesians 5:21-33 is, without a doubt, the most frequently quoted — and misquoted — portion of Scripture regarding how a man and woman should relate to each other in marriage. However, we sometimes miss its full meaning because we fail to consider its context. Considering the context is one of the most important rules of interpretation of any literature, including the Bible. In this case, it has to do with where we begin our reading, that is, where the paragraph or thought unit begins. Since the original Greek manuscripts did not always include such text divisions, there are differences of opinion as to whether the new thought starts with verse 21 or 22. How does one decide?

Fortunately, the grammar of verse 22 provides a clue. In the earliest and most reliable collections of New Testament Greek manuscripts (Nestlé-Aland and United Bible Society editions), this verse contains no verb. Despite this fact, virtually every modern English translation inserts one. But in doing so, they must borrow the verbal idea from the participle "submitting" in the previous verse. In fact, one must look back to Paul's command at the end of verse 18, "Be filled with the Spirit!" to find the foundational statement for the single sentence in verses 21-22.

For those of us who are not grammarians, this simply means that the idea of "submitting to each other" as believers — including that of wives to their own husbands — is just one part of what Paul means by being filled with God's Spirit. Thus, a literal translation of Ephesians 5:18b, 21-22 would read, "Be filled with the Spirit...submitting to each other out of reverence for Christ — wives, to your own husbands as unto the Lord."

Two points are clear: (1) the submission of a woman to her own husband in marriage is just one side of the mutual submission God requires of both partners; and (2), mutual submission of a husband and wife is an expression of being filled with God's Spirit.

Paul's call to believers at Ephesus to "submit to each other" is similar to the twelve statements of mutuality in marriage he made to the Corinthians (1 Cor. 7; discussed in chapter 4), as well as many more "each other" statements in his letters. Consider carefully this representative list:

| | | |
|---|---|---|
| Romans | 12:5 | Be united with each other in one body. |
| | 12:10 | Be kind to and honor each other. |
| | 12:16 | Show humility toward each other. |
| | 14:13 | Do not judge each other. |
| | 14:19 | Strengthen each other. |
| | 15:5 | Have a Christ-like attitude toward each other. |
| | 15:7 | Welcome each other. |
| | 15:14 | Hold each other accountable. |
| | 16:16 | Greet each other affectionately. |
| 1 Corinthians | 12:25 | Care for each other. |
| Galatians | 5:13 | Serve each other. |
| | 6:2 | Bear each other's burdens. |
| Ephesians | 4:2 | Be patient with each other. |
| | 4:25 | Be truthful with each other. |
| | 4:32 | Forgive each other. |
| | 5:21 | Submit to each other. |
| 1 Thessalonians | 3:12 | Abound in love for each other. |
| | 4:18 | Comfort each other. |

Do you think it's safe to say that mutuality between believers in the Christian community is a central theme in Paul's writings? Indeed it is! In Ephesians, Spirit-filled mutual submission is the general principle (5:18, 21), which is then applied in slightly different ways to wives and husbands in a marriage relationship (5:22–33).

So, yes, "mutual" does mean what you think it means! In the church, it means humbly serving others rather than seeking our own rights. In marriage, it carries the connotation of yielding to each other in a way that benefits both partners and harms neither. It is truly a "win-win" model for both marriage and ministry!

## Does "submission" mean that he's in charge?

Faculty members at the school of theology where I teach often get into academic debates while enjoying a cup of coffee. My wife thinks we're kind of nerdy that way, somewhat unable to talk about "real life." And, quite often she's right. But, in one case both goals were accomplished.

Years ago, a former seminary teacher and now a colleague of mine, was discussing with me the meaning of the Greek term translated in Ephesians 5:21 and 24 as "submit." Moreover, we were asking how this command should impact our marriages. Even now I can still recall his comment. He said quite confidently, "When God specifically calls wives to submit to their husbands, this implies that husbands have authority over their wives."

But after further thought, it seemed that such an assumption flies in the face of Paul's call for submission to "each other" in the very same sentence. Encouraging both partners to practice mutual submission cannot logically be construed to mean that in the end one must be in charge of the other. Rather, it's more like what we saw in chapter 7, where Paul explicitly called both wives and husbands to yield authority to each other "in the same way" (1 Cor. 7:4). In these texts, yielding authority and submitting are, for all practical purposes, synonymous. Neither action automatically invests the other partner with authority.

For example, a couple of colleagues of mine decided to share the pastoral responsibilities of a local church near our school. In this kind of leadership structure there is no "senior pastor" (who, by the way, doesn't have as much authority as one might think). Rather, they routinely yield to each other, partnering together to shepherd their flock as true "associate" pastors.

Likewise, in 1970, my wife Pat and I started a wedding photography business in order to help pay my way through my graduate studies. Since it was my idea to begin the business, I might have demanded the right to be the "senior partner." Instead, we decided to work together as equal partners in a context where each voluntarily submitted to the other. And, it worked quite well for the two decades we ran the business!

By its very nature mutual submission does not put one person in charge of another. On the contrary, it calls each partner to yield his or her own rights and voluntarily submit to each other as a service to Christ. It is a way for both wives and husbands to demonstrate that they are followers of Jesus, who once yielded his authority in order to serve and sacrifice for the church (Phil. 2:5–8; Matt. 20:28). This is why the wife is called to yield "in reverence to Christ" (Eph. 5:21) and "as the church submits to Christ" (5:24), and slaves are called to submit "as unto the Lord" (6:7). It is a voluntary act of yielding in love, the wife's way of fulfilling her part of the mutual submission command at the beginning of this passage.

But, you might ask, what about the husband? How does he obey the call to mutual submission? And, why does Paul call him the "head"?

## Did Paul just turn "male headship" on its head?

Paul's words to both wives and husbands in verses 22–33 play off the idea of male "headship," which has its roots as far back as the judgment of the first couple in Genesis 3. Remember, after the fall, God said that Eve would desire to master Adam, but in the end he would rule over her (Gen. 3:16).

Male headship, also known as "patriarchy," has been found in almost every society since. Paul readily acknowledges this reality in his own Greco-Roman culture when he says, "The husband is the head of the wife" (5:23). It is his starting point for applying the principle of mutual submission to the husband, which will radically turn certain assumptions about male headship upside down.

Though it might sound a bit out of place in modern western culture, a call to wives to submit to their husbands in Paul's day would not have raised an eyebrow for Jews or Greeks. This is why his words to the wives are so few. Young teenage girls at that time were often given in marriage to men as much as twice their age. The husband was then expected to take the place of his new wife's father and help her complete her growth to maturity. For a child-bride to submit to an adult-husband in that culture would have simply made sense to the original readers of this letter.

However, Paul's words to husbands, which make up most of this passage, would have been far more controversial. And, to the surprise of many today, they are not identical to those sermons we often hear at weddings. There is no mention here of a husband "taking spiritual leadership," "being responsible for," or "making final decisions." Sure, this kind of hierarchy was common in those days, and still occurs today in many marriages. But, the Bible never endorses it—neither in this letter nor elsewhere. Rather, as my colleague Michelle Lee-Barnewall likes to say, Paul turns "headship on its head" in the passage.

Paul acknowledges patriarchy, as he does the authority of slave-masters, but he does not condone or encourage either. In other words, he does not tell husbands to "act as the authority over." Rather, he goes on to give specific instructions as to how they should live within that cultural structure. The critical question is, "What does the apostle call husbands and masters to do with their privileged positions?" For the slave-master Philemon, it was to stop treating Onesimus as a slave and start treating him as an equal—indeed as a brother in Christ (Philemon 16). For husbands in the church at Ephesus, it was to live out the greater principle of mutual submission with their wives by loving them sacrificially as part of what it means to be filled with the Spirit (Eph. 5:18b, 21–22).

Pastor and author Charles Swindoll used to say in his Sunday morning sermons, "You can't make an analogy get down and walk on all fours." In other words, analogies have a specific point to make and should not be applied too broadly. Here the husband's relationship with his wife is compared to that of Christ's relationship with the church, of which he is the Savior. Our Lord Jesus lived a sinless life in order to be the perfect sacrifice for the sins of all who would believe. However, this is obviously not true of husbands — not even the best of us!

So then, what lesson is Paul drawing from the "Christ-church" analogy? His main point is straightforward and clear: Christ loved the church in such a way that he was willing to sacrifice his life for her well-being (5:25–27). This single point is presented here as an example for husbands to love their wives sacrificially, even as they love their own bodies (5:28–30). Men, if you forget everything else that's being said here, remember this one thing. In the long run, it will revolutionize your marriage.

In the Greco-Roman household codes of Paul's day, wives were usually put in the same category as children and slaves. The idea of the husband (master) of a household in this context loving his wife sacrificially would have come across as radical. In fact, the very notion of cutting off the "head" to benefit the "body" (in a physical sense) would have sounded completely absurd. But then so would Jesus' call for his disciples to die to themselves in order to gain real life in his kingdom (Matt. 16:25). In fact, the idea of the Son of God humbly serving humanity to the extent of dying for its sins (Phil. 2:5–8) topples prevailing paradigms of power and authority in the ancient world as well as the contemporary.

Ephesians 1:20–23 sheds further light on what the husband is called to do for his wife. After God raised Christ from the dead, he seated him at his right hand, above all rule, authority, powers, and dominion (20–21). Moreover, he placed "all things under his feet and appointed him head over all things for the benefit of the church, which is his body, the fullness of the one who fills everything in every way"

(22–23). Clint Arnold, another colleague of mine, once brought to my attention that "head" is used in two ways in this passage: (a) "authority over" and (b) "source of benefit for." Jesus exercises authority over worldly powers in order to be a source of provision and benefit for his body the church.

But the question remains, "In which of these ways should a husband be head of his wife in Ephesians 5:21–33?" Though Paul acknowledges that husbands at that time had authority over their wives, he does not reinforce or encourage such a practice. Rather, he focuses strictly on the second meaning of "headship." That is to say, he calls husbands to act in a beneficial way toward their wives. Moreover, the husband should go so far as to give his own life in this pursuit. As Jesus taught his disciples and demonstrated in his death, there is no greater way to love and serve others than to give your life for them (John 15:13). This is how the husband is to fulfill his side of mutual submission (Eph. 5:21).

Paul concludes this powerful passage with a well known quote from the creation story: "This is why a man leaves his father and mother to unite with his wife" (Gen. 2:24; Eph. 5:31–32). Then he summarizes his instructions, "Husbands love your wives as yourselves; and wives respect your husbands" (Eph. 5:33) — notice the same balance in Paul's letter to the Colossians (3:18).

One more question: "Should such commands be understood as being gender exclusive, or only gender specific?" In other words, when the pastor of a church today chides husbands on Valentine's Day to love their wives, does this mean that the wives are excused from loving their husbands? I've never heard anyone even suggest such a thing! Yet, when the same pastor admonishes wives to submit to their husbands, it is too often assumed that this excuses husbands from doing the same in response. The call for mutual submission has been ignored far too long!

In contrast, wives should certainly love their husbands (Titus 2:1), yes, just as Christ loved the church. If necessary, a wife should even be willing to lay down her life for her husband, just as he should for her. And just as surely as wives should yield in love to their husbands, so husbands should yield in love to their wives (1 Cor. 7:1-6). This is the kind of mutual submission Christ wants for his church in general — and it is just as true for believers who are married.

For centuries, women living in patriarchal societies have sought to balance the scales through a pseudo-submission that in reality turned out to be a not-so-subtle manipulation. As a modern proverb puts it, "He may be the head, but she is the neck that turns the head any way she wants." Manipulation, however pragmatic, is not the way of Christ and has no place in Christian marriages.

Instead, Ephesians 5:21–33 is a beautiful picture of how mutual submission applies in marriage. The commands are gender specific in order to address the specific needs of each spouse in a particular situation like ancient Ephesus. For wives, it meant that the freedom in Christ (which Paul had written about earlier in Gal. 3:28; 1 Cor. 7) should not lead to defending rights or usurping authority. Rather, service to others — including their husbands — is still the way of the cross. For husbands, it meant that being "head" was no longer about exercising authority as master of the household. Like Philemon with Onesimus, men should give up the traditions of power and control in order to love and serve others — including their wives — sacrificially.

## Reflection and Discussion

1. How would you define "mutuality" in light of the many "each other" statements discussed in this chapter?

2. How many relationships have you been in (not just marriage) where one person assumed that he or she was in charge? When has "yielding authority" not resulted in one person being put in charge?

3. What does "mutual submission" in marriage mean to you in practical terms? If you were to write to your church today about this, would you word it differently than Paul? If so, how?

4. Do you know of a married couple that practices mutual submission? How does their marriage differ from others that do not? How are they the same?

5. Does contemporary Western culture help or hinder husbands and wives in mutually submitting to each other? How so?

6. How do 1 Corinthians 7 and Ephesians 5 work together to form a more comprehensive view of mutuality between husbands and wives?

7. How do ideas like yielding authority, mutual submission, and sacrificial love apply to our lives outside of marriage? Give some specific examples.

# — 6 —

# Sharing God's Gracious Gift of Life
### 1 Peter 3

> Wives, submit to your husbands so that, if they are not yet believers, your pure and reverent lives will win them over. Husbands, do the same, in consideration and respect of your wives as co-heirs of God's gracious gift of life (1 Pet. 3:1–7).

In our third and last chapter in the section on mutual submission in marriage, we turn to an excerpt from a short letter written by the apostle Peter and circulated among Jewish exiles across several Roman provinces in what is modern Greece, Turkey, and beyond. Peter's concern is that these believers live in a godly manner even though they often suffer persecution under their pagan rulers. In 1 Peter 3:1–7, he speaks specifically to wives and husbands about their personal behavior under these circumstances.

## What if my spouse is not yet a believer?

In chapter four of this book, we discussed briefly the question of interfaith marriage. In both of his letters to the believers in Corinth, the apostle Paul specifically instructed his readers that if they chose to marry, it should be only to other believers (1 Cor. 7:39; 2 Cor. 6:14–18). This was based on the Law of Moses (compare Ezra 10:2; Neh. 13:27) and a lesson that should have been learned from King Solomon (1 Kings 11:1–6).

But as you already know it doesn't always work out this way in practice. Sometimes people marry outside of the faith without realizing that this is wrong. Others, sadly, choose to do so with full knowledge of the Bible's teaching. If you fall into one of these two categories, don't despair! We serve a God of grace and forgiveness even when we as Christians fall short of these virtues. In yet other cases, people marry before either one of them comes to faith in Christ. Afterward, one of them becomes a believer while the other does not.

If you see a reflection of your own marriage in any of these situations, take heart, because these words are for you! And even if you are happily in a marriage with another deeply devoted Christian, there is still much to be learned from this passage.

Peter's advice to wives and husbands is set against the larger context of Christians suffering under pagan Roman oppression. These Jewish believers in Christ are called to live such godly lives that even unbelievers in authority over them might come to faith (1 Pet. 2:11–12). Again, the operative term is "submit," as it was in Ephesians 5:21. First, they are told to submit to earthly authorities, such as the Roman emperor and his regional governors (1 Pet. 2:13–14). Second, slaves are told to submit to their masters, and are even given the example of Christ who suffered terrible injustices for them (2:18, 21). Third, wives are told to submit "in the same way" so as to win over a non-believing husband (3:1). And finally, believing husbands are told to act "in the same way" toward their Christian wives, living with them in a kind and understanding way as heirs together of God's gracious gift of life (3:7).

When I read this passage in my university class, I almost always get the same reaction: "Must I submit in everything? Are there no exceptions? What if my husband beats my children and me? What if he forces me to do immoral things, or even worship pagan gods?" Thankfully, the answer can be found in two biblical illustrations: one in the teaching of Jesus and the other in the testimony of Peter himself.

The first is found in Mark's gospel (7:1–23), where Jesus is engaged in a dispute with the Jewish religious leaders of his day. These Pharisees and scribes had criticized him and his disciples for not following the traditions they had added to the Mosaic Law. Jesus replied, "You have set aside God's Word in favor of the traditions of men (7:7, 9)." Patriarchy is the result of human fallenness as well as a "tradition of men" like those Jesus was facing. It is not a creation mandate and does not require a wife's blind obedience.

The second illustration is similar. It comes from a story in Acts 5:12–42. Peter, who had quickly risen to a significant leadership position in the infant days of the church, is preaching in Jerusalem near the Jewish temple. Because he is declaring Jesus to be the Messiah, some of the Jewish religious leaders arrest him and bring him before the Jewish Sanhedrin (high court). Peter's response is simple and direct: "We must obey God rather than mere mortals!" In the end, Peter and his companions walked away happy to have been counted worthy to suffer for Christ.

The same principle that Jesus invoked in response to criticism from the Jewish religious leaders of his day, and the same one that Peter used later in his defense before others from the same group in Jerusalem, can also be applied to Peter's call to submit to earthly authorities in 1 Peter 2–3. In fact, we all are urged to live at peace with others — including spouses — as much as it depends on us (compare Rom. 12:18; 1 Cor. 7:15). But, if it becomes unreasonable for conscience sake, and we have exhausted all possible options, then I believe both Jesus and Peter would say, "Obey God over mere mortals!" (Acts 5:29).

Domestic abuse is far too common in our so-called civilized societies, and the numbers are still unacceptably high among conservative Christians.

Moreover, we have only recently begun to address the problem. For the record, 1 Peter 3:1–7 should never be used to condone such an ungodly practice, especially when it's done in the name of male leadership rights!

With this important exception clearly in mind, let's consider Peter's words to wives married to husbands who are not yet believers. He instructs them to yield to their husbands by living pure and reverent lives (1 Pet. 3:2). They are to draw their beauty from the gentle and quiet spirit within that is so precious to God, rather than depending on hair, clothing, and jewelry (3–4). Their hope in God should be evident in the way they respect their husbands, as it was with Abraham's wife Sarah (5–6).

This advice is powerful for all of us — women and men. Yes, these words, like those in Ephesians 5 are gender specific, but not gender exclusive. For example, what makes all of us truly attractive to others in general (not just wives to husbands)? How can we all present the gospel of Jesus Christ in an attractive way to others in a pagan or secular culture? Peter's answer is a pure and reverent life, a quiet and gentle spirit, respect for others, and hope in God. What strikes me deeply as I write these words is how much they describe the model that Jesus gave us!

## Should men ever submit to women?

Way too often we get hung up on whether wives should submit. In contemporary jargon, "This is a no-brainer." The Bible clearly tells wives to submit (Eph. 5:21; 1 Pet. 3:1). What we usually miss, however, is that it also tells husbands to "do the same" (1 Pet. 3:7) There is only one verse directed at husbands in this passage, but it is powerful. Yes, guys, this section is for you!

Remember our discussion in Chapter 5 of this book about the missing verb in Ephesians 5:22? If not, take a minute and review the first section (Does "mutual" mean what I think it does?) because we have a similar situation here in 1 Peter 3:7.

Literally, the sentence reads, "Husbands, in the same way [do something...] living with them and understanding them as being weaker, honoring them as your partner in inheriting God's gracious gift of life, so that your prayers won't be hindered." The missing verb at the beginning of the verse begs the question, "Husbands, in the same way do what?"

The way most Bible translations answer this question (with slight variances) is to express the verbs as commands. This is to say, "Husbands, in the same way, live with your wives...understand them...honor them." Though this solution is common, it leaves the reader wondering why Peter prefaced the command with "in the same way."

Peter Davids, a friend and New Testament scholar who specializes in the letters of the apostle Peter, recently made a better suggestion. As it turned out, it was something that I had been pondering myself for a while but only in very rough form. Since the dominant theme in this passage is "submit" to civil authorities, slave-masters, and husbands (2:13–14, 18; 3:1), and since the phrase "in the same way" specifically had been applied to submission for wives (3:1), then it seems most likely that the writer wants us to understand the same idea of "submit" in connection with the phrase "in the same way" directed at husbands (3:7). The implication was clear in Ephesians 5:21–22 and makes the best sense here. The full thought would be, "Husbands, in the same way submit to your wives, living with them, understanding them, and honoring them."

Some women athletes are probably thinking, "All that sounds good to me; but what's this about women being weaker?" That's a good question. In fact, a young friend of ours named Brittany Watrous recently completed a grueling triathlon (also know as an "ironman" competition). It's an all-day race of swimming (2.4 mi), cycling (112 mi) and running (26.2 mi) that leaves many participants (men and women) lying along the side of the road. Anyone want to call Brittany a "weak" woman? And, by the way, never tell a mother who has successfully endured twenty-three hours of labor with her first child that she is weaker than her husband who fainted along the way!

Yet, in Peter's day, women were not permitted to participate in athletic games, were generally far less educated than men, and could not wield the same degree of social power. Even today, men and women generally compete in separate events in the Olympics and elsewhere—although some women are breaking these and other barriers.

Peter's point is not that women are somehow internally weaker than men (though generally men have more upper-body strength). Rather, he is telling husbands, who usually enjoy a greater degree of power and authority, not to use that advantage over their wives. Rather, husbands are to submit to their wives "in the same way" that wives should submit. For husbands it means being considerate and understanding—in other words honoring their wives as heirs in partnership with them of God's gracious gift of life. In fact, "partner" comes from the old Anglo-Norman French "parcener," which means "joint-heir," the very same concept emphasized here!

## *Women and men as heirs together: Is there a catch?*

Consider two other biblical pictures of the principle of women "sharing the inheritance" of God's gracious gift of life with men.

The first comes from what is possibly the oldest writing in the Bible, the Book of Job. In the epilogue to this famous story of tragedy, suffering, and faith, God finally encourages his righteous servant Job who had remained faithful through a truly incredible ordeal. As the narrator puts it,

> The Lord blessed Job's elder years more than his youth, giving him seven sons and three daughters. His daughters' names were Jemimah, Keziah and Keren-Happuch. They were the fairest in the land! Moreover, Job made them heirs along with his sons (Job 42:12–15).

Normally, in the patriarchal world of Job, daughters received no inheritance — unless there were no surviving sons. This was the case with Mahlah, Tirzah, Hoglah, Milkah, and Noah, the daughters of Zelophehad in Numbers 35:1-13. But in Job's extraordinary case a blameless and upright, God-fearing father decided to give his daughters an equal share with their brothers as "heirs together" of the family estate. And, it is equally surprising that only the names of Job's daughters are given in the account (not the sons). What a kind word of encouragement for them in their patriarchal world!

The second is a word-picture from Galatians 3:26–29, a passage we discussed earlier in Chapter 3. As you may recall, Paul had just declared that all believers were "children of God through faith" regardless of ethnicity, social status, or gender. Then he concludes, "If you belong to Christ, you are Abraham's descendants and heirs according to the promise" God made to him. Religious privileges were inherited through men throughout the Old Testament. But, Paul declares, in the body of Christ things have changed. Gender is now irrelevant for inheriting the privileges and promises of God.

Yes, men and women are meant to be "heirs together" in God's gracious gift of life — there is no caveat to be added! In fact, this wonderful truth is not just intended for married couples because Galatians includes the entire community of God's people — all the brothers and sisters. Remember, God designed us that way in the beginning as "suitable partners" (Gen. 2:18). Peter simply applies this general truth to husbands and wives.

So what are the implications of Peter's words? Yielding to each other in love is the overriding principle in marriage. It's not about one person having authority over the other. Rather, it's about both partners voluntarily surrendering their rights in honor of the other. It's having the same attitude toward each other that our Lord had when he surrendered his divine privileges to become a humble, human servant in order to suffer and die for our sakes (Phil. 2:5–8). As Peter puts it, the submission of Christ in his suffering was intended as an example for other believers to follow (1 Pet. 2:21).

## Reflection and Discussion

1. Wives, is your husband not yet a believer? Look carefully at your life. Does he see you as "attractive" in the way Peter defines it—in a way that will draw him closer to a personal relationship with your Savior?

2. Are you in an abusive relationship with your spouse? Have you considered every option available to you to improve the relationship? Are you doing what is necessary to keep yourself and your children safe right now?

3. Do you know a couple going through a marriage crisis? How could you become an instrument of love, grace, and forgiveness for them? Are you willing to stay connected with them through the long, hard struggle?

4. What do you think it means for women to be "weaker vessels"? Are there exceptions to the rule in some cases? Are men weaker in certain areas? What special responsibilities come to mind when you think of being a "stronger vessel"?

5. In your experience, what non-biblical caveats have sometimes been added to the biblical principles of women and men being co-heirs (such as, inheriting most but not all privileges)? In contrast, what would an equal partnership as "heirs together" look like?

6. How do the examples of Jesus in Philippians 2:5–8 and 1 Peter 2:21 specifically inspire godly living by believers like you and me? Be specific about what Jesus did and how we can follow in his steps.

# Principles for Today

Both the apostles Paul and Peter affirm what we have discovered in the redemptive history from creation to the cross: an equally shared partnership where mutual submission is the operative principle. This is an especially powerful statement when the cultural context of their day is considered. In both Jewish and Greco-Roman households, women were generally given in marriage as soon as they were able to bear children—and usually to men as much as twice their age (for example, a thirty-year-old man might take a wife in her early teens). In this context, it is no surprise that the young wife was expected to submit to her more mature husband as she had done to her father, especially in matters of faith. For the apostles to call for mutuality, even between two partners of relatively equal maturity, would be a surprise at this time. But, to do so without qualification regarding differing levels of maturity reflects a radical critique of the ancient patriarchal system in terms of one-another theology.

In chapter four we discovered that the apostle Paul repeatedly described marriage as a mutual partnership between a man and a woman, with an emphasis on yielding one's own rights and authority to the other (1 Cor. 7). He spoke with tolerance and grace whether he was addressing singleness, marriage, or divorce. Yet, he made it clear that those who choose to enter into something so intimate and sacred as marriage should take it seriously and share it only with another believer.

In chapter five, we considered Paul's call to wives and husbands to submit to each other out of reverence for their Lord and as evidence of being filled with the Holy Spirit (Eph. 5). Though no further explanation was necessary for wives at that time, this was radically different for the husbands from anything they had ever known. Specifically, the husband was to express his side of mutual submission by loving his wife, even to the extent he would love his own body. The "headship" the husband was accustomed to enjoying had suddenly been stood on its own head.

In its place, the way of Christ was set forth as the model for Christian husbands, that is, the way of yielding rights and privileges in order to humbly serve their wives.

In chapter six, we examined the words of the apostle Peter, who advised wives to yield in love — within reason and conscience — even when their husband is not yet a believer (1 Pet. 3). They were called to emulate godly examples of women like Sarah so that their witness for Christ could be revealed from within, through a pure and quiet spirit. Though Peter is brief in his remarks to Christian husbands, his words, like Paul's, are radical and powerful. Husbands, likewise, are to submit to their wives by being considerate and respectful of them as heirs together to God's gracious gift of life. Yes, as Paul had declared earlier (Gal. 3:29), women were to be viewed as full and equal partners with men, joint-heirs of all of God's promises.

So, what should a biblical picture of marriage look like?

First, notice that we have not encountered any mention of patriarchy (that is, male leadership) in the creation accounts (Gen. 1–2) or in the letters of Paul (1 Cor. 7, Eph. 5) and Peter (1 Pet. 3). That is to say, the Bible never endorses a male-leadership model for marriage. It just isn't there! Does this mean that a marriage cannot have a leader? Not necessarily. In fact, in most marriages one spouse often exhibits more leadership skills or tendencies than the other (though it is not always the man). Spouses should be sensitive to the different ways and areas in which they each might take initiative or give direction on different occasions.

Second, the cultural "headship" that Paul recognizes in his day and works within is never prescribed as something Christians should perpetuate. That is to say, husbands are never instructed to "be the head of" or "exercise authority over" their wives. Moreover, neither spouse is called to "take the lead" or "be responsible" for the other by making "final decisions." Rather, as the old saying puts it, "Christ is the head of every household." We could bring significant healing to our broken marriages in contemporary society by taking this truth more seriously.

Conflicts will always occur, but our testimony to the world — as well as our marriages — would be so much stronger if we humbly submitted ourselves to each other, as well as to our Lord.

Third, the biblical model for marriage is a partnership of equals with each spouse making his or her unique contributions. This is evident in creation design and confirmed in Paul's bold declaration to the churches of Galatia regarding our oneness in Christ (Gal. 3:28). Moreover, it is reinforced in Paul's letters to the churches in Corinth (1 Cor. 7) and Ephesus (Eph. 5), as well as in Peter's letter to the churches scattered across the Roman provinces (1 Pet. 3). We need to develop the attitude that Jesus had when he let go of his authority and gave us the model of genuine servanthood. Ironically, by doing so he empowered others to follow his example.

Finally, we need to love each other sacrificially. In doing so, we must remember that in the Bible love is always an action word. It is more about commitment than chemistry. That is not to say we shouldn't enjoy and celebrate God's gift of marriage with all of its pleasures. In fact, I'm all for it! But, we must realize at the end of the day that we don't just "fall in love." Rather we choose to love even as our Lord chose to love us. Romance may begin a marriage relationship, but commitment sustains it through the inevitable crises of life.

# PARTNERS
*in Ministry*

# — 7 —

# Celebrating our Uniqueness as Women and Men
### *1 Corinthians 11*

I entered my teenage years in 1959, at a time when traditional styles were about to be thrown into an upheaval. My folks had danced to Frank Sinatra and the "big bands" until Elvis Presley came along and changed all that. By the 1960s, folk music legends like Bob Dylan and Joan Baez were leading us into yet another era of social revolution. The customs and traditions, including those regarding ethnicity, social status, and gender, would be challenged in new ways. As a young believer and student of Scripture, I wondered how we were going to separate essential biblical principles from specific cultural applications. Thankfully, Paul spoke to similar concerns in his first letter to the church at Corinth. His words were helpful then and remain so today.

Earlier we discussed "Yielding to Each Other in Love" from 1 Corinthians 7 and discovered the apostle's strong emphasis on mutuality in matters of singleness, marriage, and even divorce.

Here in 1 Corinthians 11 Paul turns his attention to the practice of traditional dress and hairstyles when women and men serve together in the "up-front" positions in church.

## Does it really matter who came first?

The Twentieth (XX) Winter Olympic games took place in 2006 in the snowy Alpine villages around Torino, Italy. As you know, this level of competition is all about "who comes in first." It's of little concern to most that the top ten contenders in the downhill skiing all arrived within seconds of each other. In fact, many in the United States were outraged when the American snowboarding contender Lindsey Jacobellis made a mistake and only took the silver medal. The news media was brutal. It was as if they could only say the glass is .01% empty instead of 99.9% full! But, in the end, only three persons stand on the podium (out of the hundreds who thought they might) and only one gets "Olympic Gold."

As we discovered in Genesis 2, Adam "came in first" before Eve — perhaps only hours after him if the creation days are to be taken literally. More importantly, she came from his body, just as all human beings thereafter would come from her (she would be their "mother"). Each was the "source" or "point of origin" for humanity in his and her unique way. In creation, God made a deliberate statement of balance that was different from what we find in athletic competition. Eve doesn't remain second, but becomes the first for the rest of humanity. This kind of mutuality was important in God's creative design and, as we will learn from 1 Corinthians 11, also mattered greatly to the apostle Paul.

Paul shaped this passage in such a way that the key points are set in parallel groups with the strongest emphasis appearing at the center. The following chart will serve as a helpful point of reference as we discuss the passage.

| | |
|---|---|
| **A** | Regarding the traditions: Christ the head of man, man the head of woman, and God the head of Christ. |
| | **B** A man who prays or prophesies with his head covered dishonors his head, while a woman who does so with her head uncovered dishonors her head. |
| | **C** Man is the image and glory of God, and woman the glory of man. Woman came from man, and was made for man. |
| | **D** For this reason *a woman ought to have authority over her own head* because of the angels. |
| | **C** Nevertheless, in the Lord women and men are not independent. For as woman came from man, so also man comes from woman — and everything comes from God. |
| | **B** A woman should cover her head when praying. Nature shows that a man's long hair is disgraceful, but a woman's long hair is her covering. |
| **A** | We have no other practice — nor do the churches of God. |

Paul begins his remarks by praising the Corinthians for keeping the traditions that he passed on to them during an earlier visit (11:1-2, 16). Then, he uses the imagery of "headship" to make a new point. As he did in his letter to the church at Ephesus, Paul utilizes the metaphor in a creative way — he stands it on its "head" again. In Ephesians 5, he started with the common cultural assumption of "male headship" including "male authority," then dramatically turned the idea upside down emphasizing in its place mutual submission in terms of a radical and sacrificial love — yes, specifically from husbands.

Paul makes a similar play on words here, though this time he nuances the other common idea of male "headship" in terms of "source" or "point of origin," such as the "head" of a river. Examples of this are found in both creation accounts. In Genesis 1:1, the word usually translated "in the beginning" is literally "at the head." Then, in Genesis 2:10-11, a water source feeding the Garden of Eden separates into four "headwaters" (in effect, "sources") that in turn feed the Pishon, Gihon, Tigris, and Euphrates rivers.

Similarly, in the patriarchal culture of the Old Testament, fathers of Hebrew households were regularly referred to as "heads" because they were considered the "source" of the many smaller clans that came from them (for example, Exod. 6:13, 25). The idea of "head" meaning "source" or "point of origin" is easily established in Scripture.

In 1 Corinthians 11, Paul employs a similar kind of "point of origin" imagery to emphasize the essential unity between men and women—like what we discovered in the "from-one-flesh, to-one-flesh" narrative of Genesis 2. He starts by explaining that "the head of every man is Christ" (1 Cor. 11:3), most likely referring to Christ's role in creation. As the apostle John put it,

> The Word [Christ] was in the beginning [in Genesis, "at the head"] with God, and was in fact God. Through him [that is, Christ, the creative Word of God] all things were made [including Adam] and without him nothing was made" (John 1:1–3).

Christ is the head of every man as the Creator because he is the "source" or "point of origin" of the first man Adam. The gospel writer in Luke 3:38 speaks in similar terms when he lists Adam as the "son of God" (that is, God was his "source" or "point of origin" in contrast to an earthly father or mother).

Paul extends his use of creation imagery in 1 Corinthians 11:3 with his second comparison, "the head of woman is man." Just as Adam came from Christ the Creator of all things, so Eve was taken from Adam (Gen. 2:18–25). This is probably what the writer of Genesis 6:1–8 means when he refers to men at this early time in human history as the "sons of God" and women as the "daughters of men" (that is, woman was taken from man).

In his third comparison, Paul steps back to see the bigger picture by declaring, "the head of Christ is God." Perhaps it seems surprising to you that Paul's order was not "woman-man, man-Christ, Christ-God" (thus, implying a hierarchy with God the Father at the top). But, the apostle is not making that point here — in fact, nowhere does he make that point. Instead, his order is, "man-Christ, woman-man, Christ-God." This follows solid New Testament Christology by associating Jesus with the creation of man and woman "in the beginning" (John 1:1-3) and declaring without contradiction that Jesus later "came from God" in the incarnation (John 13:3).

Taken together, the three comparisons in 1 Corinthians 11:3 are representative of Paul's recurring theme of mutuality. In other words, both women and men come from God (Gen. 1:26-27) even though the man was created first and the woman was taken from him (Gen. 2). Paul's all-inclusive reading of the creation and procreation orders is reinforced in the center sections of this passage (1 Cor. 11:7-12). Yes, it's true that woman was created second and for the sake of the man's aloneness (Gen. 2:18; 1 Cor. 11:7-9). However, it's also true that neither man nor woman is independent of the other, for as woman came from man so men are born of women and everything comes from God (Gen. 2:20; 1 Cor. 11-12). Paul's interpretation of the Genesis creation accounts and the main point he is making from them are clear: the orders of creation and procreation speak of mutuality with diversity. The two "orders" are meant to be set side-by-side.

"Okay," you're saying, "Enough theology! Let's get back to the practical advice Paul is giving!" Well, as he did in Ephesians 5, the apostle starts here with a common notion of male headship, but ends up in a very different place. Certainly, the Corinthian men would have said "Amen!" when they read, "the head of woman is man." In fact, I've heard similar responses from contemporary men (perhaps some of you reading these words are saying, "Amen!"). But imagine how the puffed up male ego of Paul's patriarchal readers would have deflated when they were reminded that every one of them had come from a woman, and that both men and women should be mutually interdependent (1 Cor. 11:11). This is the overall impact the apostle wanted his words to have. He intended to bring balance to the one-sided patriarchy of his day.

## *Who cares about hair and clothes?*

Having laid the theological foundation of gender interdependency, Paul turns to a more pragmatic concern: head coverings. As a child, I was brought up in the Church of the Brethren denomination. It was an offshoot from the Mennonite Brethren that had split from the old Amish order in the Pennsylvania and Ohio area. In our local church, most of the women still wore a head covering during services — some all the time. This custom, which is still practiced by conservative Mennonite and Amish women today, draws its biblical support from 1 Corinthians 11. In fact, our son's teacher in a Brethren Christian elementary school in Southern California would always cover her head when leading her second grade class in prayer.

It was also customary in Paul's day for women in "the churches of God" (1 Cor. 11:2, 16) to cover their heads, and for men to keep their heads uncovered. Moreover, the apostle instructs them to follow this traditional practice when praying or prophesying in church gatherings of that time (11:4-7, 13-15). His primary point of respecting customary gender markers is clear. However, the precise circumstances behind Paul's words are not. There are at least four possibilities as to what these "head coverings" were: (1) modest veils, then commonly worn by women; (2) some kind of a man's prayer shawl that was not normally worn by women; (3) longer hair as a "covering" for women while men wore shorter hair; or (4) an inappropriately feminine hair style for men, literally hair "hanging down on the head" (1 Cor. 11:4).

Regardless of how we understand the precise nature of Paul's reference to hair and/or headcovering, the fundamental issue for Paul at hand is that men and women should present themselves in a way that honors their gender uniqueness—especially when they are up front in church. Moreover, they should do this in a way that is respectful in the surrounding culture. For example, when my wife and I led university groups to Israel and Palestine, we would have to help our American students make the transition to a Middle Eastern culture. One point of practice was head coverings—especially for men. When we were at Jewish religious sites men needed to put their hats on, while at Christian sites they took them off. For women, the rules were different.

So, should hair and clothes really matter that much for Christians today? Well, yes and no. On the one hand, what really matters is the heart—that is, whether a woman or man is truly ministering to God's people with a sincere, heartfelt devotion to Christ. Old cultural traditions and customs should always take second place to these more important issues. They should not be used to judge another's spirituality or to exclude someone from fellowship with other believers.

On the other hand, how we dress or wear our hair can sometimes get in the way of our ability to minister or another's ability to hear us—especially in a public setting. Again, please understand that I'm not just talking about "professional" ministers! For example, it would be perfectly fine to wear a swimsuit at a pool party with your youth group; but you would be probably be more effective if you put something over it while giving a devotional talk later that evening. Or, it might be okay to wear shorts to church in Southern California—but not in the Middle East! Matters of general decency or even simple cultural preferences should never be allowed to distract from the message being preached.

But, you might be thinking, "In my cultural setting things are quite different from first century Corinth." Well, yes and no. For instance, homosexuality was quite common in the Greco-Roman era, as it is becoming again in the Western world of our own day. Similarly, people in both ancient and modern cultural settings sometimes dressed or wore their hair in a way that signaled their "sexual orientation." In the face of this, Paul clearly condemns the practice of homosexual behavior (read his tough words in 1 Cor. 6:9 and 1 Tim. 1:10). This is just one reason to take the biblical principle of beneficial gender differences seriously (our uniqueness as men and women) and apply it sensitively in the context of our own "traditions and customs."

But, celebrating gender uniqueness doesn't mean that boys wear "blue denim shirts" and girls wear "pink lacey dresses." In fact, these would get in the way of most ministry opportunities today. Nor does it mean that all women must act in the same "cookie-cutter" way in order to follow someone's definition of "femininity/womanhood" (the same holds true for men and "masculinity/manhood"). Recent studies have shown that there is considerable diversity among men, in some cases even more so than between men and women (and, the same holds true for women). The point is to retain appropriate gender markers and to put aside things that distract us or become distractions to the people we love and serve.

## So, can women preach in church?

Here we come to the central verse of this passage, 1 Corinthians 11:10. Quite literally, it comes at the "center" of the centered structure of the apostle's argument (review the chart on p. 85). This kind of structure was common for Jewish rabbis in Paul's day, steeped in the Hebrew literature of the Old Testament. In fact, entire books are arranged this way (for example, the books of Micah, Daniel, and Esther). Here, the climactic punch line is, "It is for this reason that a woman ought to have authority over her own head because of the angels." Let's unpack his cryptic yet powerful statement piece-by-piece.

First, exactly what is Paul's command to the women who were praying and prophesying in the assemblies at Corinth? Literally, the text reads, "a woman ought to have authority over her own head" (NIV) — not a "sign" or "symbol" of authority as the ASV, NASB, and ESV add. What does this mean? Every other reference in the New Testament where the phrase "authority over" occurs speaks of the authority that the subject of the sentence possesses over the object. For example, Jesus' disciples had "authority over" demons, diseases, and cities (Luke 9:1, 17); in the end-times the saints will be given "authority over" the nations (Rev. 2:26); and, God himself will exercise "authority over" the plagues (Rev. 16:9).

In the church at Corinth, Paul speaks specifically to the women who are "praying" (leading public worship) or "prophesying" (preaching the gospel) in front of the church assembly. These women leaders are to have or exercise "authority over their own heads." This could mean one of three things. One, it may mean something as simple as letting women decide how they wanted to "cover" their literal heads — that is, which hairstyle or external covering they prefer. Or, two, perhaps Paul is reminding the women to exercise that authority and keep their heads covered. Or, three, since Paul specifically acknowledges that the husband is the "head" of the wife at the beginning of this discussion (1 Cor. 11:3), his advice to the women prophets may carry forward his recurring theme of mutuality. In this sense, the apostle would be reminding the privileged male leader of the Roman household that when his wife speaks as a prophet, she speaks with authority over her "head" meaning her husband.

Whether Paul was endorsing the right of a woman prophet to choose her head covering, calling her to cover her head, or validating her authority as a spokesperson for God (like Deborah to Barak in Judg. 4–5, or Huldah to Josiah in 2 Kings 22; 2 Chron. 34), it is clear that women were serving as worship leaders and prophets in the New Testament church. Moreover, they were doing so with the apostle's blessing and even with a divinely given sense of authority.

Second, what is the reason for Paul's command? Remember, in a centered structure one must look on both sides of the main section. In this case, 1 Corinthians 11:7-9 and 11-12 complete the larger thought. As we saw above, these verses speak of the mutual interdependence of men and women as illustrated in the creation-procreation orders. Thus, the apostle reasons, (a) it is because man came first in creation and (b) because women come first in procreation that (c) a woman worship leader or prophet ought to have authority over her head. In other words, his advice to the women is linked directly to the idea of rebalancing patriarchy into mutuality. Though the men generally ruled in the household in that day, men and women could equally share leadership in the church.

The other reason given here is "because of the angels." Even though there are almost as many interpretations of this little clause as there are interpreters, we dare not ignore the apostle's words. To me, it seems most reasonable to connect "the angels" with the fact that many of these women were prophesying. In the Bible, as well as in much of the extra-biblical Jewish literature at this time, angels were the ones who mediated prophecy. In other words, they communicated God's Word to the prophets who in turn communicated it to God's people. We find this in several of the later books of the Old Testament (for example, Dan. 8-12; Zech. 1-6). Therefore, because women prophets were empowered by angels they ought to have authority over their own heads.

So, to answer the question, "Can women preach in church?" Paul would say, emphatically, "Yes! And they should do so with authority over their own heads." It surprises many modern readers that the idea of a woman preaching in church is perfectly fine with Paul. But this is not the apostle's main point in this passage. Rather, he is concerned that both men and women exercise their leadership gifts — with appropriate authority — while presenting themselves in a manner that celebrates the uniqueness of their respective genders. The cultural markers for this will vary widely from time-to-time and from place-to-place, but the principle endures. Although our appearance should not be dictated by the culture around us, we should be sensitive to how we appear within that context — especially regarding those to whom we minister.

## Reflection and Discussion

1. If you were raised in a church context, what traditional or customary "gender roles" were associated with being a Christian? Were these clearly connected to biblical principles?

2. What unique contributions do women make on the leadership team at your church? If women are not presently welcomed at that table, try to imagine what it would be like if that were to change.

3. Have you ever sat under the preaching of a woman, either pastor or visiting speaker? How did you feel about it? Why? What unique contributions do different women make (for example, content, delivery style, and sensitivity to her audience)?

4. How could you use hair and dress styles to enhance your ministry to others? What examples come to mind where these issues hindered someone's ministry?

5. Is the practice of homosexuality becoming more common in your social circles? How can churches be more welcoming of individuals with this orientation that are sincerely seeking Christ, without affirming their lifestyle?

6. How can church leadership best balance the idea of having some authority over the congregation with the principle of servanthood modeled by Jesus (compare Matt. 23:8-11 with 1 Pet. 5:1-4)?

7. Though Paul does not flinch at women prophets addressing the assembly or leading in public prayer, we often do. What practical steps could your church take to make the transition smoother for women in "up-front" ministries in church?

# — 8 —

# Leading Together with Humility, Respect, and Hope
*1 Timothy 2*

Men, stop arguing and lift your hands in prayer! Women, dress modestly and learn with quiet respect instead of teaching the men in a domineering way! And remember, women, you'll be kept safe through childbearing if your lives demonstrate faith, love and holiness (1 Tim. 2:8–15).

Just as frequently as Ephesians 5 is cited in support of patriarchy in the home, Paul's words in 1 Timothy 2 have been used to prevent women from partnering on an equal basis with their brothers in Christ on leadership teams in today's churches. And, I must sadly admit, I used to be among those who perpetrated this injustice. However, as I have studied this passage more carefully over the years in its original context, I have been surprised by what I found, as well as by what I have not found!

Paul's two letters to his "child in the faith" Timothy, were written against a rich Greco-Roman backdrop when the great apostle was in a Roman prison nearing the end of his life (AD 61–63). At that time, young Timothy served among the leaders (literally, "overseers") in a church that Paul had helped establish in the city of Ephesus. His first letter is written out of concern for the spiritual well-being of this congregation in a decadent pagan culture. More specifically, some in the congregation were teaching heresy taken from pagan myths (1 Tim. 1:3–4), and the most popular show in town was the cult of the moon goddess, Artemis.

## What had these women gotten themselves into?

Probably the last thing you expected to find in a book like this was a section on Greek mythology. Frankly, I'm a little surprised to be writing one! Yet, a brief introduction to this once dominant religion in Ephesus is essential for understanding the apostle's words in his letter to believers in this congregation.

Perhaps you've been fortunate enough to visit the extraordinary marble statue of Venus in the Louvre; or, maybe you are old enough to have danced to Frankie Avalon's first "million-dollar single" in 1959 by the same name? Either way, almost everyone has heard of Venus, the Roman goddess of love and beauty (also know in Greek as Aphrodite).

But far fewer have heard of the Greek goddess Artemis (known as Diana to the Romans), though, if you had lived in Ephesus in the first century her name would have been a household word. Futhermore, it appears that many of the women in the Ephesians church at the time of Paul and Timothy had been influenced by this pagan cult—or perhaps were even deeply involved with it. In fact, given the weight of the evidence, it's hard to imagine otherwise.

The ancient historian Antipater of Sidon (second century BC) judged the solid marble temple of Artemis in Ephesus to be the greatest of the "Seven Wonders of the Ancient World" (relegating the famed Pyramid of Cheops, Nebuchadnezzar's Hanging Gardens, and the Colossus of Rhodes all to second-class status). This impressive structure was first built in the sixth century BC, then later restored after the death of Alexander the Great. It covered more than 95,000 square feet—four times the size of the Parthenon in Athens. Moreover, it boasted exquisite

Ionic capitals that towered sixty feet into the sky atop 127 columns, many of which were etched with detailed scenes from Greek mythology.

As the most beloved goddess of ancient Greece, Artemis was portrayed as a virgin who neglected modest dress and behavior while roaming the forests with her nymphs to protect animals and children against the wiles of men. Such men, whom she generally shunned, were never able to tame her. In fact, armed with her bow and quiver she was ready to kill any man who lusted after her beauty. Both eunuch priests and chaste priestesses served in her temple as part of a powerful matriarchal cult. In addition, the common people of her day often honored Artemis in sexual orgies as a scantily clad virgin who promoted promiscuity.

Other artists of that day depicted Artemis as a many-breasted, semi-human goddess of fertility. Besides being the fearless virgin huntress, she provided fertility to women and delivered safely through childbirth those women who trusted in her. She was known as the "Mother of all Creatures," a pagan distortion of Eve the "Mother of all Living" (Gen. 3:20). However, unlike Eve, she had not been created from a man.

Okay, you're probably saying, "What does all of this have to do with 1 Timothy 2?" Stay with me a little longer while we consider the biblical account of Paul's personal encounter with the cult of Artemis.

In Acts 19:23–20:1, Paul is visiting Ephesus on his third missionary journey (AD 54–58) when he meets Demetrius, who made personal shrines for worshippers of Artemis. This Greek entrepreneur greatly feared the loss of his livelihood because of Paul's ministry. On one occasion, he even went so far as to incite a riot against the apostle and his co-workers. He claimed that such preaching would discredit Artemis' Temple and rob the goddess who was worshiped throughout the then known world of her divine majesty. The chaos spread rapidly across the city with angry mobs chanting, "Great is Artemis of the Ephesians!" In the end, the early missionaries barely escaped with their lives.

A few years later, with this vivid memory in mind, Paul wrote his first letter to Timothy concerning the church in Ephesus and their involvement with pagan myths like that of Artemis (1 Tim. 1:4).

## What does Paul have to say about this—and why?

It is always a good idea to let the larger context and the clearer statements shed light on the portion of a text that is under debate. Paul's concern here is not as much to set general principles for all time as it is to address specific problems that existed in this church at this time. Again, a chart of Paul's comments can help us see the big picture.

| Vv. | Positive Principles | Vv. | Negative Prohibitions |
|---|---|---|---|
| | Men | | Men |
| 8a | Pray with holy hands lifted high | 8b | …instead of angry arguments. |
| | Women | | Women |
| 9a, 10 | Dress modestly…with good deeds and holy living | 9b | …instead of flashy, expensive jewelry and clothes. |
| 11, 15 | Learn with quiet respect. Practice hope, faith, love and holiness | 12-14 | …instead of a domineering style of teaching (let Eve's example humble you). |

In contrast to what we saw in Ephesians 5, Paul addresses the men of the church first in this letter—and ever so briefly. He wants them to stop their angry debates and instead raise holy hands to God in prayer (1 Tim. 2:8). This is in keeping with his general principle of living peaceful, quiet, godly, and holy lives (2:2). But it also reflects his concerns about the false teaching going on in Ephesus (1:3–4). Apparently, these men were more interested in arguing about the problem than praying about it. In response, Paul instructs them to let go of their pride, to humble themselves, and to seek God's answer rather than boasting about their own ideas.

When I was a student in graduate school, my wife Pat visited one of my classes, which in that day was "men only." The first thing she said when we got into the car to drive home was, "Why do you guys always argue so much? You come across as being disrespectful of each other—even of your professor." I've never forgotten the lesson I learned from her that day. And, men, though you're anxious to read on to the "juicy part" in the verses that follow, take a moment and reflect on how you come across when discussing theology, especially in a group of guys. Does the image of "boys behaving badly" come to mind?

Now, let's take a look at what Paul says to the women. Again, though he speaks specifically to women, his advice in not gender exclusive. Rather, it can be applied to men also.

First, the women were to dress modestly, with decency and respect, instead of flaunting elaborate hairstyles or expensive clothes and jewelry. They were to "clothe themselves" with the kind of behavior that characterizes godly women (1 Tim. 2:9–10). Paul's words are reminiscent of the ancient Hebrew sage's reflections on the woman of wisdom in Proverbs 31:30: "Charm is deceptive, and beauty is fleeting; but a woman who fears the Lord is to be praised" (NIV). Moreover, they are similar to Peter's instructions to wives with unbelieving husbands in 1 Peter 3:3–4, as well as his instructions to "elders" to clothe themselves with humility (1 Pet. 5:5). And, they mirror the counsel Paul gave believers in general at the church in Colossae when he called them to clothe themselves with compassion, kindness, humility, gentleness, and patience (Col. 3:12). The principle of dressing respectfully and modestly in contrast to flaunting wealth and appearance is just as relevant for men as for women, both then and now.

Paul also instructs these women to learn with quiet respect (1 Tim. 2:11) rather than teaching in a domineering way over the men (12). The fact that the apostle instructs the women "to learn" in this passage is far too often overlooked. As in Galatians 3, here he invites women to "sit at the table with the men" so that someday they might become disciples like Mary of Bethany (Luke 10:38–42), teachers like Priscilla (Acts 18:24–26), or even apostles like Junia (Rom. 16:7). Further, learning with respect would have applied to all learners in Paul's day regardless of gender. But neither learning by itself nor learning with respect is the issue at hand here. Rather, it is learning with respect in contrast to teaching in a way that is domineering toward men.

Teaching in the days of Jesus and Paul certainly carried with it some degree of authority. Our Lord recognized this when he told his disciples to avoid the prideful behavior of the Jewish religious leaders who loved exalted titles like "rabbi, teacher, father, and master" (Matt. 23:8–12). Similarly, Gentile rulers loved to "domineer" or "lord it over" their subjects (Matt. 20:25). In sharp contrast, Jesus' followers were to shun these prideful temptations and humble themselves for the purpose of service instead (26–28).

Paul seems to have this sense of prideful teaching in mind in 1 Timothy 2:12 when he prohibits the women at Ephesus from teaching. The second prohibition in verse 12 reinforces this idea. It is best translated, "to usurp authority" (KJV), "to assume authority" (NIV), or "to domineer" (NEB). The softened renderings "to have authority" (NKJV) or "to exercise authority" (NASB) miss both the strength and tone of the original term, which in Paul's day was strongly negative. So, the complete thought is that Paul does not want these women to teach in a way that domineers or usurps the existing leadership, which at that time was mostly composed of men.

But, you might be thinking, why does Paul specifically direct these instructions to women? Wouldn't it be just as wrong for men to do this? The short answer is, "Yes, it would be." But, a more complete answer can be found in the examples he cites and the promise of hope that follows, which are all taken from Genesis 2–3. Paul first reminds these women that their ancestor Eve both came from a man and was deceived by the serpent (2:13–14). Then, he assures them that they will be kept safe through childbearing if they are sincere in their faith, love others, and live holy lives (15). His intent was to humble their pride, yet at the same time to sustain their hope.

So, why drag Eve into this? To begin with, the word "For" at the beginning of verse 13 conveys the idea "for example." Eve is being used as an illustration through which these women can humbly recognize the error of their way. But, we might ask, aren't there other examples in the Bible of prideful women who were deceived that might have been used instead (say, Delilah or Jezebel)? It is important here to take into account the influence of the Artemis cult on the women of Ephesus. Paul's concerns about false teaching involving pagan myths (1 Tim. 1:4) certainly would have included memories of the cult he had encountered so dramatically not too many years earlier (Acts 19).

Likewise, Paul's prohibitions against women teaching in a domineering way make better sense when set in the context of the Artemis cult where the pagan goddess encouraged women to dominate men. Further, Paul's examples of Eve's creation and deception would humble the women's prideful assertions that Artemis did not come from a man and did not need men. Finally, the apostle's promise of hope regarding safety in childbirth provides godly women the assurance that Eve's judgment of "painful toil in childbearing" (Gen. 3:16) should be addressed not in Artemis, but in Christ.

## So, can women share in church leadership?

The big picture that Paul is painting throughout this passage is one of contrasts between positive principles and negative prohibitions (review the chart above). Men are to pray instead of argue. Women are to focus on godly character instead of flaunting wealth, status, and appearance. Likewise, women are to learn with respect rather than teaching in a domineering way. In all three contrasting pairs, Paul calls his readers to pray, learn, and serve with humility instead of proudly or arrogantly promoting their own agenda. And, in each case, the positive principles, as well as the negative prohibitions, could and should be applied today to both men and women.

Whenever I read this passage, I am reminded of our many family vacations in the Amish area of Lancaster County, Pennsylvania, not far from the rural community in which I grew up. In fact, when Pat and I visited there a couple summers ago, I picked up a little booklet called "A Quiet and Peaceable Life." The title is a quotation from 1 Tim. 2:2, KJV). The "plain people" (as they like to call themselves) use this passage even today to preserve a strictly conservative lifestyle of dress, hair, and behavior that dates back to eighteenth century Europe. Most of their practices are not specifically prescribed in Scripture, but are carried forward from their culture instead. So it is with the notion of "men only" as leaders in today's churches. While the early church had mostly men in its leadership (for example, notice the gendered language of 1 Tim. 3:1–7 regarding elders and deacons), it also allowed for women leaders like Priscilla and Junia to serve. In other words, it was not exclusive like many churches are today. More importantly, as Christians, we are not called to preserve the cultural norms of early centuries. Rather, we are to take the principles that are clearly taught in Scripture and apply them with wisdom in our ever-changing cultures.

So, once again the answer to the question is an emphatic, "Yes!" Godly and gifted women can and should share leadership responsibilities with men in the church or home. Paul's specific application of a biblical principle to the women at Ephesus should not be misread or misapplied as a generally restrictive rule for women in all times and places. After all, why should we do this with only one of the three contrasts he makes? We don't require men to raise their hands in prayer nor prohibit women from wearing nice clothing and jewelry, or braided hair. But, we must call men and women to prayer instead of fighting, to modesty instead of pride, to learning with respect instead of dominating others. When we hear this message, we will have heard Paul's heart from this passage.

## Reflection and Discussion

1. Try to imagine living in Ephesus when Greco-Roman mythology like the cult of Artemis was the order of the day. How might that perspective have affected your reading of this passage?

2. If you are a woman, have you ever been tempted to replace patriarchy with matriarchy, that is, to do unto men what they have done unto you? If so, how did you deal with that temptation?

3. Have you ever been guilty of arguing instead of praying? In general, is this more of a problem with men? Would it help to have more women involved in theology?

4. Are valuing wealth, personal appearance, and learning in a respectful way still a problem in today's churches? Is either of these more of a problem for women than men? Vice versa?

5. Does teaching in a contemporary church carry with it a degree of authority? What would be a good example of this? How about a bad one?

6. Have you ever witnessed a situation where someone has taught in a domineering way in your church? Was it a man or a woman? What was the result?

7. If you are a woman, have you ever needed to be humbled by a negative example like Eve's behavior in Genesis 3? How might Adam's failure be used to humble prideful men?

# Principles for Today

I'm often asked, "Can women be elders, pastors, or even senior pastors?" Usually, my response is, "You're asking the wrong questions." In contrast, let's ask, "What are the biblical requirements for serving in church leadership?" And the answer from Scripture is "godliness, giftedness, experience, and education." These issues are addressed directly and clearly.

In contrast, the Bible nowhere speaks of a "senior pastor" (man or woman), nor does it ever restrict women from serving as elders or serving among the "shepherds of a flock" of believers alongside their brothers in Christ. In fact, the idea of women in public ministry, preaching, or teaching, is only addressed in two biblical passages, and then only as a tangent.

In chapter seven, we found that some women in the church at Corinth were ministering as prophets (spokespersons for God's word to God's people). In today's churches we would probably think of them as preachers. In his first letter to these believers (1 Cor. 11), Paul expressed two concerns for these women: one, that they should be sensitive to cultural "gender markers" in their appearance (then, "head coverings"), and two, that they should have "authority over their heads" when they pray or prophesy. Neither of these commands restricted women from preaching. Moreover, both are applicable today, though they probably would be applied in different ways. Remember, in giving these instructions Paul is careful to bring balance to the patriarchy of his day by reminding his readers that just as woman came from man so also men come from women—and ultimately we all come from God. The principle is gender mutuality expressed in the orders of creation and procreation.

In chapter eight, we examined a different situation: the men and women of Ephesus, a city heavily influenced by the pagan Artemis cult. First, Paul instructed the men to pray instead of fighting. Then, he told the women to dress modestly and do good deeds instead of flaunting their wealth, status, and beauty. Finally, the women were to learn the way of Christ with quiet respect instead of teaching in a domineering way over the men (1 Tim. 2).

Paul also humbled the proud Ephesian women with illustrations of Eve being taken from Adam and being deceived by Satan—the latter leading humanity into transgression. Neither of these instructions prohibited mature and godly women who were well educated in the Bible from teaching men in an appropriate way at a later time and in a different situation. Nor should this passage be used today to prevent women from sharing leadership responsibilities with men. In fact, the apostle's words once again have something to say to both men and women, both then and now, though the same principles may be applied differently in different contexts.

So what does all this mean for women in contemporary church settings? Several principles for personal application can be drawn from these two passages.

First, like the early Christians under Roman rule, we also live at a time when sexual intimacy between members of the same sex is relatively common. We should be welcoming to men and women of this orientation that are earnestly seeking to follow Christ. Yet, we cannot affirm their lifestyles in light of clear and strong statements of Scripture (for example, Rom. 1:26; 1 Cor. 6:9).

In contrast, we should celebrate our God-given and beneficial differences as men and women. Yet, at the same time, we should acknowledge the many ways in which we are similar, that is, "corresponding partners" who both came from Eden (Gen. 2–3). No doubt, this also will manifest itself in a variety of ways peculiar to the individual men and women involved. And, since the Bible does not define "femininity/womanhood" or "masculinity/manhood," we should avoid dogmatism, stereotyping, and the making of restrictive lists in these areas also.

Second, we must be careful how we use "authority" in our preaching and teaching. Pastors and preachers speak with a legitimate sense of authority only to the extent they represent God's Word. Ultimately, the authority is God's, not ours. However, we can easily be tempted to assume that we have authority in ourselves as leaders and attempt to domineer others. Since even Christ did not cling to his authority (Phil. 2:5–8) neither should we cling to ours. As the Master himself put it, "So you also, when you have done everything you were told to do, should say, 'We are unworthy servants; we have only done our duty'" (Luke 17:10, NIV).

Third, when choosing church leaders, we should focus more on matters of godliness, giftedness, maturity, and learning, instead of gender, social status, and ethnicity. Moreover, the pride that often is attached to titles and offices should be shunned. Elders in the New Testament who were "shepherding the flock" are always spoken of in the plural with none designated as the "head shepherd" (or, "senior pastor"). Even the great apostle Peter, the "rock" with the "keys of the kingdom" (Matt. 16:18–19), recognized that in the end he was merely a "fellow elder" serving alongside others with only Jesus as the "Chief Shepherd" (1 Pet. 5:1–4). Thankfully, many churches today have embraced a more biblical model of "team leadership" that adapts to the gifts and maturity of the individuals involved.

Finally, godly and gifted Christian women today should be encouraged — not merely allowed — to participate in church leadership alongside their brothers in Christ. Don't get me wrong here, this is not about feminism; it's about mutually equal partnership. As men, we need to invite our sisters to "sit at the table" with us, to learn with us, and indeed to join us as servant-leaders to the congregation. Our sisters in Christ need our full support and encouragement just as we need theirs. This is not a time to be silent or passive. Rather, it is a time to speak out with affirmation and conviction!

# Paths to the Future

As we have seen, the Bible consistently teaches gender mutuality, from Adam and Eve to the ministry of Jesus, as well as in the writings of both Paul and Peter. All of these passages point to a complementary partnership of equals where leadership responsibilities are shouldered together in a community of oneness. The New Testament presents us as a new people of God in which the old barriers of ethnicity, social status, and gender are declared irrelevant in the context of unity in Christ (Gal. 3:28). Though we've come a long way over the history of the church in reaching this biblical ideal, we're not there yet. There are still many churches that insist on perpetuating an ancient patriarchal system (though to varying degrees of softness and in steadily declining numbers).

In such a context, how can we journey together to help the church move forward toward a more biblical ideal? I believe the answer is threefold: one, we must believe that change is possible; two, we must be willing to get involved personally; and three, we must move forward being fully aware of what's at stake.

## Is change really possible?

The inspired writer to the Hebrews warns us in the great "Hall of Faith" that if we are to come to God, we must believe that God exists and that God rewards earnest seekers (Heb. 11:6). Sincere faith engenders hope that change can take place.

On my journey, I have studied the "gender question" now for over thirty years. And, during this time I have witnessed some significant changes at the Christian university where I teach, as well as in the churches where my wife and I have ministered. Yet, the wheels of progress in this area have ground at a tediously slow pace at times. Occasionally I have wondered, "Is there really hope?"

When this kind of doubt rears its ugly head, I turn to the end of the gospel accounts and read the resurrection narratives. I remind myself that if God can raise Jesus from the dead — the foundational event of our faith — then God can also bring oneness to the church, even regarding the gender debate. In other words, I believe change is possible because I believe in the resurrection of Jesus Christ.

I'm also reminded of Paul's words in his second letter to the Corinthians. There he declares that the church is a "new creation" through which we have been reconciled to God. Moreover, we have been given "a ministry of reconciliation" (2 Cor. 5:17–19). Reconciliation is a divine mandate for all of God's people, not an option. It is the essential component in the ministry to which everyone in the church is called.

The questions are still daunting: "Is God able to restore unity to the body of Christ regarding the gender debate?" Yes! "Can God knock down the barriers that we have set up between men and women?" Yes! "Can I pray and expect God to stir the hearts of Christian couples toward mutual submission, sacrifice, and honor as joint-heirs?" Yes! "Is the partnership that is so evident in the creation design still achievable today?" Yes! "Can God bring true brotherhood and sisterhood among the leaders of our churches in place of the patriarchy that has dominated for so long?" Yes! The answer in every case is a resounding "Yes!" God is both willing and able!

## *What can I do personally?*

God brings about change in the church through ordinary individuals like you and me who respond to God's Word and Spirit. One person can influence a couple of others who eventually form a coalition of the willing. Here are some practical steps that you can take to promote a model of mutual partnership in your home and church.

First, change must be biblical. Remember that Jesus Christ is the model for our behavior toward each other. Paul's words to the Philippians are worth repeating: "Have the same attitude toward each other that

Jesus Christ had. Though he was God, he relinquished his divine rights in order to become a mere mortal, indeed a humble servant who was willing to die like a criminal on a cross" (Phil. 2:5–8). Solving the gender problem is not about demanding our rights; it's about servanthood. For over 2,000 years, this has been the way of the cross.

Second, change involves both women and men. We must keep in mind that in the end, this is a biblical equality movement, not merely a women's movement. It's about mutuality and partnership, not matriarchy or feminism. Even in our moderately patriarchal western society today, men generally have control of power positions. As in the first century, this continues to be the lay of the land today in the home, the church, and the workplace. This is why Paul also calls men to mutual submission (Eph. 5:21), to love and sacrifice for their wives (Eph. 5:25–28), to defer to them in love (1 Cor. 7:4), and to submit to them by treating them as joint-heirs in life (1 Pet. 3:7). Though mutual submission includes the wife, her influence can only go so far to change the nature of a marriage relationship. The most significant change often has to come from the one with power. The "head" must be willing to sacrifice for the body (Eph. 5:25). In other words, husbands need to let go of their assumed authority and become true servants in the context of mutual submission.

This same principle holds true in the church, where men still hold the majority of leadership positions. The way of Christ is not to push oneself into leadership, but to serve (1 Tim. 2:11–12). Where leadership is needed, those brothers with the responsibility of oversight should invite their sisters to join them on the leadership team. In churches with a congregational form of government, both women and men can be involved in promoting this by way of the congregational vote. Women who have been pushed down and out for so long need to be encouraged and empowered to serve alongside their brothers in Christ. Jesus did this for Mary of Bethany, and Paul did it for the apostle Junia. As men in today's churches, we can do no less!

Third, change takes time and patience. For many in the church, the biblical idea of mutual partnership between men and women is still unfamiliar territory. They are used to the more familiar patriarchal model. Often I hear someone say, "It seems strange to see a woman preaching. Though the Bible doesn't say she can't do it, the whole thing just doesn't feel right to me." How can we help such persons move forward toward a more biblical model of equality in Christ?

In our own local church, it has helped to encourage women to participate more frequently in visible, up front activities where they are accepted. These may include things like leading in prayer, reading Scripture, leading congregational singing, making announcements, ushering, taking up the offering, serving communion, sharing their experiences in spiritual growth, and/or serving on the deacon board (just to name a few). As people get used to these, they will eventually become more comfortable with considering a woman's voice on the elder board or with hearing someone call a woman "pastor." Even though such changes are right because they're biblical, it still takes time for people to adjust to them. And while this is happening, we must practice the virtue of patience.

Fourth, change requires a sustained effort. Paul also encouraged the church at Galatia — the same folks who were struggling with the Jew vs. Gentile issue — not to become weary in doing good, for at the proper time they would reap a harvest if they did not give up (Gal. 6:9). Doing what is right can be hard work. It can wear you out on a good day and on a bad day leave you downright depressed. We live in a world of instant remedies. We're told we can lose weight in just days and make a fortune overnight. We're assured that we can have what we want when we want it — and at a bargain price.

Patriarchy has marred male-female relationships since the day Adam and Eve were driven from the Garden of Eden. In the name of patriarchy, women have been abused for thousands of years — even Christian women with believing husbands. In addition, women have been excluded from sharing leadership with men throughout most of church history. God's creation design that was marred by our sin has been in need of repair for a long time. And, it's not going to be fixed in just a decade or even a century, though contemporary efforts toward truly biblical equality over the past two centuries have turned us in the right direction. While we must be patient, the twenty-first century is no time for giving up or remaining silent! In God's time, we will reap a great harvest if we stay at the task. And be assured, God will vindicate those who cry out from the margins of the church on behalf of those who have no voice!

## *What's at stake?*

Several years back, I was having breakfast with my former academic mentor from my PhD program. When he inquired about my current writing projects, I told him of the work I was doing on *Discovering Biblical Equality* (InterVarsity, 2005). His response was, "Oh, how trendy!" Other friends have also joked about my efforts in this area as being "politically correct." But, an important issue like this cannot be trivialized so easily.

For one last time, review with me Paul's words to the Galatians, especially the tone and intensity of his appeals. He begins by expressing his astonishment at how easily these believers deserted the gospel of grace in order to follow a false and perverted gospel. He even goes so far as to sentence such persons to God's curse. Then, he declares that his intent is to win God's approval—not that of people—for he is a servant of the Messiah who gave him this message. The great rabbi emphasizes his Jewish background and his persecution of the church because what he is about to say will come as a shock to many of his Jewish readers (Gal. 1:6–24).

Paul had been called by God to be an apostle to the Gentiles, just as Peter was to be an apostle to the Jews (Gal. 2:1–10). Knowing that they might not react kindly to this radical inclusiveness in a predominately Jewish church, Paul cites an encounter where he publicly rebukes Peter and other Jews for not eating at the same table with Gentiles. He goes so far as to call such exclusiveness "hypocrisy" (2:11-13), that is, "not acting in line with the truth of the gospel" (2:14). "Oh foolish Galatians," he asks, "who has bewitched you? ...You began with the Spirit. Why are you now trying to finish by human effort?" (3:1, 3). This is the foundation Paul lays for his famous declaration that all believers are children of God through faith, regardless of ethnicity, social status, or gender. Indeed, these old divisions are no longer relevant in a church where Christians live as a unified community of heirs together to God's promises (3:28).

For Paul, the oneness of all believers without the old social barriers was at the very heart of living out the gospel message. To acknowledge a so-called "equality of spiritual status" without applying that truth in the everyday activities of home and church was hypocrisy. In fact, it was out of line with the truth of Scripture. Instead, the Galatians were "turning back" to become slaves again to that from which Christ had freed them (Gal. 4:9). The great apostle is perplexed with their behavior, just as he is zealous about his conviction. He even likens his struggle with them to the painful struggle of women in childbirth (4:12–20).

In the end, Paul calls both men and women to stand firm in the freedom to which Christ has called them (Gal. 5:1–2, 13). He explains that because we first came to life by God's Spirit, we are to "walk by the Spirit" (5:16), and "keep in step with the Spirit" (5:25, NIV). This means we must live out the reality of our spiritual standing before God in our relationships with each other if we are to honor the gospel message.

This is what's at stake: honoring women as full partners with men in both the home and church! Mutual partnership was present in God's design of men and women when humanity was first formed. Moreover, it continues to stand at the very center of the gospel message of Jesus Christ. The apostles Paul and Peter endorsed this biblical ideal in spite of the patriarchy of their day. To stand firm in this freedom is to reflect their message. To do so with passionate conviction and a servant's heart is to follow their example as well as that of Jesus.

# For Further Reading

Ruth Haley Barton, *Equal to the Task: Men and Women in Partnership* (Downers Grove, Ill.: InterVarsity Press, 1998).

Carol E. Becker, *Becoming Colleagues: Women and Men Serving Together in Faith* (San Francisco, Calif.: Jossey-Bass, 2000).

Gilbert Bilezikian, *Beyond Sex Roles: A Guide for the Study of Female Roles in the Bible* (Grand Rapids, Mich.: Baker, 1985).

Loren Cunningham and David J. Hamilton, eds., with Janice Rogers, *Why Not Women? A Biblical Study of Women in Missions, Ministry, and Leadership* (Seattle, Wash.: YWAM, 2000).

Jonalyn Grace Fincher, *Ruby Slippers: How the Soul of a Woman Brings Her Home* (Grand Rapids, Mich.: Zondervan, 2007).

Rebecca Merrill Groothuis, *Good News for Women: A Biblical Picture of Gender Equality* (Grand Rapids, Mich.: Baker, 1997).

Patricia Gundry, *Heirs Together: Mutual Submission in Marriage* (Grand Rapids, Mich.: Zondervan, 1980).

Mark Husbands and Timothy Larsen, eds., *Women, Ministry and the Gospel: Exploring New Paradigms* (Downers Grove, Ill.: InterVarsity, 2007).

Alan F. Johnson, ed., *How I Changed My Mind about Women in Leadership: Compelling Stories from Prominent Evangelicals* (Grand Rapids, Mich.: Zondervan, 2010).

Craig S. Keener, *Paul, Women and Wives: Marriage and Women's Ministry in the Letters of Paul* (Peabody, Mass.: Hendrickson, 1992).

Catherine Clark Kroeger and Mary J. Evans, eds., *The IVP Women's Bible Commentary* (Downers Grove, Ill.: InterVarsity Press, 2002).

Alice P. Mathews, *A Woman God Can Use* (Grand Rapids, Mich.: Discovery House, 1990); *A Woman Jesus Can Teach* (Discovery, 1991); *A Woman God Can Lead* (Discovery, 1998).

Alvera Mickelsen, ed., *Women, Authority and the Bible* (Downers Grove, Ill.: InterVarsity Press, 1986).

Ronald W. Pierce and Rebecca Merrill Groothuis, eds., *Discovering Biblical Equality: Complementarity without Hierarchy* (Downers Grove, Ill.: InterVarsity, 2005).

Glen Scorgie, *The Journey Back to Eden: Restoring the Creator's Design for Women and Men* (Grand Rapids, Mich.: Zondervan, 2005).

Aída Besançon Spencer, *Beyond the Curse: Women Called to Ministry* (Nashville: Thomas Nelson, 1985; reprint Peabody, Mass.: Hendrickson, 1989).

Sarah Sumner, *Men and Women in the Church: Building a Consensus on Christian Leadership* (Downers Grove, Ill.: InterVarsity, 2003).

Steven R. Tracy, *Mending the Soul: Understanding and Healing Abuse* (Grand Rapids, Mich.: Zondervan, 2005).

Ruth A. Tucker, *Women in the Maze: Questions and Answers on Biblical Equality* (Downers Grove, Ill.: InterVarsity Press, 1992).

Mary Stewart Van Leeuwen, *Gender and Grace: Love, Work and Parenting in a Changing World* (Downers Grove, Ill.: InterVarsity Press, 1990).

# About the Author

Ron and Pat married in 1969. They live in Southern California where Ron has taught Bible and theology at Biola University since 1976.

They have two children: Debi with her husband Dan, and Brett with his wife Sarah. They also have four grandchildren: Zachary, Matthew, Heidi, and Kristen. Debi is a partner in an accounting firm, while Dan is a full-time, stay-at-home dad. Brett and Sarah each have their own careers as an IT manager and CPA respectively.

Ron holds academic degrees from John Brown University, Talbot School of Theology, and Fuller Theological Seminary, and is an ordained minister with Converge Worldwide (formally General Baptist Conference). He has been a passionate advocate for a biblical, gender equality since the late 1980s. Recently, he co-edited *Discovering Biblical Equality* (InterVarsity, 2005) with Rebecca Merrill Groothuis and Gordon D. Fee.

# About Christians for Biblical Equality

Christians for Biblical Equality (CBE) is a nonprofit organization of Christian men and women who believe that the Bible, properly interpreted, teaches the fundamental equality of men and women of all ethnic groups, all economic classes, and all age groups, based on the teachings of Scriptures such as Galatians 3:28:

> "There is neither Jew nor Gentile, neither slave nor free, nor is there male and female, for you are all one in Christ Jesus" (NIV 2011).

## Mission Statement

CBE affirms and promotes the biblical truth that all believers — without regard to gender, ethnicity or class — must exercise their God-given gifts with equal authority and equal responsibility in church, home and world.

## Core Values

We believe the Bible teaches...

- Believers are called to mutual submission, love and service.
- God distributes spiritual gifts without regard to gender, ethnicity or class.
- Believers must develop and exercise their God-given gifts in church, home and world.
- Believers have equal authority and equal responsibility to exercise their gifts without regard to gender, ethnicity or class and without the limits of culturally-defined roles.
- Restricting believers from exercising their gifts — on the basis of their gender, ethnicity or class — resists the work of the Spirit of God and is unjust.
- Believers must promote righteousness and oppose injustice in all its forms.

## Opposing Injustice

CBE recognizes that injustice is an abuse of power, taking from others what God has given them: their dignity, their freedom, their resources, and even their very lives. CBE also recognizes that prohibiting individuals from exercising their God-given gifts to further his kingdom constitutes injustice in a form that impoverishes the body of Christ and its ministry in the world at large. CBE accepts the call to be part of God's mission in opposing injustice as required in Scriptures such as Micah 6:8.

## Envisioned Future

Christians for Biblical Equality envisions a future where all believers are freed to exercise their gifts for God's glory and purposes, with the full support of their Christian communities.

## Join the Movement

CBE members are extraordinary advocates for Christ's liberation from human limitations imposed by gender, ethnicity, or class. By joining CBE, you stand together with Christians around the world who promote the biblical truth of equality. As a member, you receive cutting-edge resources on what the Bible says about gender and justice. And your dues support and sustain our ministry!

Membership benefits include: a subscription to *Priscilla Papers*, our quarterly, award-winning academic journal; a subscription to *Mutuality*, our quarterly, award-winning popular magazine; 50% off CBE-produced recordings and 15%-20% off all other resources at our online bookstore; discounts on registration to CBE conferences; access to e-versions of recent issues of our journals; and more.

Visit cbeinternational.org/membership to join today!

CPSIA information can be obtained
at www.ICGtesting.com
Printed in the USA
BVHW071047010323
659481BV00008B/646